SPEAK TO YOUR
MOUNTAIN!

Kenneth W. Hagin

Unless otherwise indicated, all Scripture quotations in this volume are from the *King James Version* of the Bible.

Fourth Printing 2007

ISBN-13: 978-0-89276-728-1
ISBN-10: 0-89276-728-6

In the U.S. write:
Kenneth Hagin Ministries
P.O. Box 50126
Tulsa, OK 74150-0126
1-888-28-FAITH
www.rhema.org

In Canada write:
Kenneth Hagin Ministries
P.O. Box 335, Station D
Etobicoke (Toronto), Ontario
Canada, M9A 4X3
www.rhemacanada.org

Contents

Contents

Chapter 1
The God-Kind of Faith
Receives the Promises of God

In the Old Testament, God told the children of Israel to possess their Promised Land. But as a New Testament believer, your inheritance in Christ is *your* promised land.

What do I mean by that? All the promises of God are yours right now. Everything your heart could ever desire is contained in the promises in God's Word. They already belong to you, but you've got to receive them by faith.

But you won't be able to receive what legally belongs to you in Christ unless you exercise the God-kind of faith. That's the kind of faith that turns impossibilities into possibilities.

Before you can claim what belongs to you in Christ using the God-kind of faith, you'll need to learn to take God at His Word. Success in life comes from believing that God meant what He said in His Word.

Some people want to put their own interpretation on the Word of God. They want to read the Bible with denominational or theological glasses on, and that can change the meaning.

There's nothing wrong with denominations or studying theology. But people get into trouble when they try to understand the Word of God without depending on the Holy Spirit of God. When people read the Bible with eyes colored by their own viewpoint, they can make the Bible say what they want it to say.

Biblical Confession

Why don't we just take God's Word for what it says? For example, in Mark 11:23,24, Jesus gave us a pattern for biblical confession and prayer. This is one way you possess all that God has for you as a believer. These scriptures show us *the God-kind of faith.*

Why do many believers have problems possessing all the promises of God for their lives? Is it that they don't *believe*? Well, usually it's that they don't *confess* God's Word before they see the answer.

In Mark 11:23,24, Jesus explained God's inevitable law of faith — the God-kind of faith. God's law of faith is to *believe* in your heart that you receive your petition when you pray. Then you *confess* with your mouth that your need is met according to God's Word. That's how you *receive* your answer by faith.

> **MARK 11:22-24**
> **22 And Jesus answering saith unto them, Have faith in God** [have the God-kind of faith].
> **23 For verily I say unto you, That whosoever shall SAY unto this mountain, Be thou removed, and be thou cast into the sea; and shall not doubt in his heart, but shall BELIEVE that those things which he SAITH shall come to pass; he shall have whatsoever he SAITH.**

24 Therefore I say unto you, What things soever ye desire, WHEN YE PRAY, BELIEVE that ye receive them, and ye shall have them.

Jesus introduces Mark 11:23,24 by saying, "Have faith in God." In the margin of my Bible it says, "Have the faith *of* God." Other translations read, "Have the faith that God gives," or "Have the God-kind of faith."

Then in verse 23, Jesus begins to explain the God-kind of faith. The God-kind of faith has to do with what you *say* or *confess*. The word "say" is used in some form three times in Mark 11:23: *say*, *saith*, and *saith*. So what you *say* is important if you want faith that works.

Evidently, Jesus was telling us that we're going to have more trouble with our *saying* than we are with our *believing*. That's one reason why it's scriptural to continue to speak the Word of God about a situation.

Many people read this passage of Scripture and say, "Well, it was Jesus doing the talking, all right. But I don't believe He meant what He said."

If Jesus didn't mean what He said — that we can have what we say — then why didn't He say what He meant? No, we don't have to try to figure out and interpret what Jesus said! In this passage of Scripture, Jesus explains to us how the God-kind of faith works.

Practical Faith

I'm a practical person, and I like to teach Bible practicalities. I want spiritual truths I can live by *now*. I thank God for the yesterdays, and I thank God for what He's going to do for me in the future.

But yesterday is gone; I can't live in the yesterdays. And I can't live in the future either. Besides, I know God will take care of me in the future just like He does in the present.

I believe in living in victory right *now* — not just sometime in the future. I need scriptural principles that work so I can receive what God has for me right now. Confessing God's Word is practical, and it works *right now* for anyone who puts it to work.

So many times when people preach and teach, they talk about how great things were in times gone by. Or they talk about the future, saying, "Well, bless God, one of these days . . ."

But, you see, the spiritual principles Jesus taught in Mark 11:23,24 are for our success right now. It's by these principles that we receive what God has already done for us.

Jesus told us how to receive our inheritance in Him now. We don't have to wait until we get to Heaven. The moment we get our faith lined up with the Word of God, the Word will begin to work for us. That's how we possess all the promises of God — it's by the God-kind of faith!

I want you to notice that there are three important points in Mark 11:23,24. First, Jesus said that the one who practices the God-kind of faith must *not doubt* in his heart.

Second, Jesus said that a person must *believe* that those things he *says* will come to pass. Third, when he *believes* God's Word in his heart and *confesses* it with his mouth, then he shall *have* whatsoever he says.

If what you say with your mouth is a result of what you believe in your heart, and it's based on God's Word, then the Word will work for you. That's how you activate the God-kind of faith or the faith that comes from God.

The God-kind of faith is how you receive everything God has promised you in His Word. *Believe* God's promise, *confess* God's promise, and *receive* God's promise.

You see, there are a lot of Scriptures in the Word of God. Many of them tell us what Christ has already done for us. So since Jesus has already bought and paid for our inheritance at the Cross of Calvary, then it's ours *now*. Think about it! We don't have to wait until we get to Heaven. The promises of God are ours now! They belong to us.

What do you have to do to get something from God that already belongs to you? How do you possess the promises? You just receive them by faith. How? By confessing the promises in God's Word and then by acting like God meant what He said. You take God at His Word. That's faith.

For example, suppose someone bought you a new car and handed you the title and the keys for it, and said, "I bought this brand-new car for you. Here's the title. The car is yours."

You'd get excited about it, wouldn't you? You'd probably go tell everyone, "I got a new car! Here's the title, and I've got the keys right here to prove it."

But what if someone asked you, "How do you know you've got a new car? Have you seen it? Have you driven it? All you have is a piece of paper. That's only someone's written word for it."

But if you've got the title and the keys — legally it's *yours!* You have a *legal* right to get in that car and drive it away.

It's the same way if you buy stocks on the stock market. You may never actually *see* the stock, but once you sign your name on a legal contract, that stock is yours. Once it's yours, you can turn around and sell that stock or do whatever you want to do with it because you've got a legal contract that says it belongs to you.

Well, God entered into a contract with us in the New Covenant. Therefore, each one of us has a legal contract with God. Our legal contract with God is the Word of God.

In order to possess what our legal contract — the Word of God — promises us, we must meet the conditions of the contract. One way we do that is by our confession of the terms of the contract. In others words, we confess God's Word.

What happens sometimes is that we believe the Word and we even confess it, but then we try to make it come to pass ourselves. But that's *God's* part of the contract. *Our* part of the contract is to believe and confess

His Word. If we do that, God will uphold His part of the contract.

Confession as Corresponding Action

Let me tell you another reason why it's necessary to confess God's Word. The Bible says that faith without works is dead (James 2:20). Another translation says, "Faith without corresponding actions is dead." So believing something without acting on it won't get you anything. Confessing the Word is one way you act on the Word. You confess it as done.

If someone gave you a car, and you believed that the car is yours, you'd get in the car and drive it off. That would be your corresponding action to your faith that the car is yours.

If God promised you something in His Word, *confessing that it is yours* before you actually see it manifested is a corresponding action to your faith.

Also, some people make faith confessions, but still nothing happens. Do you know why? Because they've never learned that if they're going to make a confession according to God's Word, they may have to add some additional corresponding action to it like getting up and doing what God told them to do!

Too many people passively say, "Oh, I believe what the Word says! The Word says I'm more than a conqueror in Christ." But because they don't put any action to their confession, they're hit by Satan's attacks, and they spend all their time dodging his fiery darts.

They claim, "I'm more than a conqueror in Christ!" Then Satan's attacks come. *Swat! Swat! Whap!* and they try unsuccessfully to dodge them.

When they try to possess the promises of God, and there's no corresponding action to their faith, they fall on their faces in defeat. But the God-kind of faith *says* and then *acts* on what it says.

You see, *believing* is only part of faith. *Confessing* is acting on your faith. It's the corresponding action to your faith. Believers usually have a harder time with confession than they do with believing, because they have a harder time understanding that faith requires corresponding action. Confession is a corresponding action.

Confession Extremes

The climax of Mark 11:23 comes when Jesus said, "You shall have whatsoever you *say*." Of course, what you say has to be based on the promises in God's Word. If you're going to run around just claiming anything, you're going to get into trouble.

So when the Bible says you can have what you say, it's not talking about just anything you say. It has to be something that's promised to you in God's Word. If the Bible says something belongs to you, then you need to talk in line with God's Word, not against it, so you can receive your inheritance in Christ — your promised land.

Some believers have acted on what they thought was "faith" and made all kinds of confessions that weren't based on the Word, and it was nothing but presumption and foolishness.

You see, God made provision for us to receive anything we need in this life, but our desires have to be in line with His Word. You can't expect God to give you something that violates His Word!

For example, you hear some believers say, "I claim this woman for my wife." Or "I claim this man for my husband." That's a bunch of nonsense! If you're single, you have a right to claim a spouse based on God's Word, but you can't claim just anyone you want!

You can't just have *everything* and *anything* you say. Yes, you can have what is promised to you in God's Word. But just claiming anything you want isn't the faith confession Jesus was talking about in Mark 11:23.

I think this is where some people have taken the so-called "faith message" to the extreme and caused confusion in the Body of Christ. I don't even like that term "faith message" because it's really just the *Bible* message. The faith message is simply the message of faith in God's Word.

Some people call "faith" people the "name-it-and-claim-it bunch." They say, "Well, I don't believe in this 'name-it-and-claim-it' business."

I don't believe in it either because it's not in line with the Word of God! Just claiming *anything* you want by faith is a bunch of nonsense. For one thing, you can't name or claim something that God hasn't already promised you in His Word.

The problem is that some believers hear one message on faith, and then they run off with it and get everything in a mess. Then it gives the rest of us a black eye, so to speak. Then people think we believe the same way — but we don't.

You can take any Bible doctrine to the extreme and cause confusion in the Body of Christ. You can't claim by faith what doesn't already belong to you in Christ.

You've got to have the Word of God to back you up. God says He will bring *His* Word — *His* promises — to pass in your life, not your own words. God doesn't back up *your* word unless it's in line with *His* Word.

But He backs up His own Word every time! God's Word says, *"If ye abide in me, AND MY WORDS ABIDE IN YOU, ye shall ask what ye will, and it shall be done unto you"* (John 15:7).

So when you talk about "naming it and claiming it," you need to name something that's promised to you in the Word and you confess what God's Word says by faith, then you have the right and the authority to receive what you're confessing.

God Himself backs up your confession when your claim is based on your inheritance in Christ. Otherwise, your words have no more meaning than "Twinkle, twinkle, little star. How I wonder what you are."

When some believers try to claim things that aren't in line with God's Word, and their faith doesn't work, it hinders them from believing that confession is scriptural.

And some people go to the extreme on confession

and get afraid to say *anything*. When you joke with them, they say, "Oh, I wouldn't say *that*! I wouldn't make that confession!"

For instance, I walked into an auditorium once where a couple of fellows were working on the sound system. I knew them, so as a joke I said to their boss, "What are you doing letting those guys work on the sound system! When they're done with it, it'll never work right!"

The man in charge said almost in fear, "Oh, don't make that confession!"

You see, that's where people take the confession teaching too far. I was just having fun with those two men because I knew them. I didn't believe that in my heart, so it wasn't a confession, and it wouldn't come to pass.

What's happened is that some people have taken the confession teaching to the extreme so that some believers are afraid to laugh and joke and have fun with each other.

It doesn't matter whether your confession is based on God's Word or whether it's a natural fact, if you state something you don't believe in your heart, it's not really a confession according to God's Word.

In order for your confession to be a biblical confession, you have to believe in your heart what God's Word says and speak it with your mouth.

Yes, it is scriptural to guard your mouth. The Bible says so (Prov. 13:3). It is important what you say. But if you're not careful, you can get yourself into bondage in this area, so you won't even be able to enjoy people! Instead of getting in a ditch on the confession teaching, let's just stay in the middle of the road.

Another confession extreme is to claim something based on someone else's testimony. For example, a fellow gave a testimony telling how he believed God and received a certain material possession from God.

Another man heard that first man's testimony, and said, "I'm going to claim one of those for myself."

I said to him, "Why are you claiming it?"

"Well, *he* did, so *I'm* going to."

I said, "You won't get it."

He said, "Wait a minute! He believed God and got it, so I'm going to do the same thing."

I asked him, "What scriptures are you standing on?"

"Well, I'm just basing it on that other fellow's testimony."

I said, "God is not in the business of making what you claim from someone's testimony come true. God didn't say to believe in your heart and say with your mouth what someone else said.

"God said to believe in your heart what *He* said, and say with your mouth what *He* said. He's in the business of making *His Word* come to pass if you claim it in faith."

Then I said to him, "What does God's Word say? John 15:7 says, *'If you abide in Me and My words abide in you; you shall ask what you will.'* If His Word isn't alive in your heart, then you're just saying words out of your mouth.

If you're going to successfully claim the promises of God for your life, you'll need to know and practice John 15:7. Why? Because if you don't have the Word of God abiding in you, you could ask amiss (James 4:3).

That's why you have to abide in God's Word so His Word can abide in you! If you're in that place of abiding with God — you commune with God and His Words dwell in you — you won't ask amiss. You won't ask out of line with God's Word.

What happens sometimes is that believers claim something they want, but nothing happens, and they don't understand why their faith isn't working.

But if their faith isn't based on the Word, they aren't really operating in *Bible* faith — they're just saying something out of their mouth, so it can't produce any results. It's the Word of God that produces results!

God doesn't promise to bring to pass what you speak out of your mind if your words aren't founded on His Word. Mark 11:23 says to believe in your *heart*, and John 15:7 says *God's Word* has to *dwell* in your *heart* before you can receive from God!

Base your faith and your confession on God's Word, and your faith will work for you. *Believe* God's Word, *say* God's Word, and *receive* what God's Word promises.

You need to realize that you are going to get in this life what you believe in your heart and what you say with your mouth. Good or bad, positive or negative, what you say and really believe in your heart, you will receive.

Many believers make a lot of so-called "faith" confessions, but they don't really believe them in their heart, so they won't receive anything from God. The biblical principle of faith is *believing* in your heart and *speaking* your conviction with your mouth.

Another area where some believers have taken the faith-confession teaching out of bounds is that they make faith statements that are nothing but lies.

We need to rip the lid off some of this foolishness that's going on right now in the Body of Christ. There's no such thing as a faith statement and a faith confession when it's nothing more than an out-and-out lie!

For example, suppose someone calls you on the phone and asks you about a bill you owe them, and you say, "Oh, the check is in the mail," but you really don't have any money. You may try to justify saying that by claiming, "I said that by faith." But that's not a faith statement — that's a lie!

How in the world do you think God is going to honor you when you're lying? You see, there's a distinction between standing your ground in faith, and lying about the circumstances. You can stand your ground on the Word, but you won't be able to stand your ground on a lie.

I've seen churches get into trouble because people made faith confessions instead of paying the bills. Then when the pastor asked them, "Did you pay the church rent?" they replied, "Oh, yes, Brother Pastor. It's all paid!"

If you'd ask them why they didn't tell the truth, they'd say, "Oh, we don't want to make a negative confession, so we're confessing our faith instead." But it's not a faith statement to say the bill is paid when it isn't — it's a lie!

When someone comes out and cuts off the electricity or locks the doors to the building, the person will find out whether his faith was based on the promises in God's Word or on presumption!

If you're making a biblical faith statement, you can say, "No, we haven't been able to pay the bill yet. But we believe God is going to meet our need and provide the funds according to His riches in glory through Christ Jesus."

Of course, believers who are really in faith are also doing all they can in the natural realm to pay their bills. Believers who won't work — don't eat! It's that simple. And if you don't set your hand to something, God doesn't have anything to prosper (Deut. 28:12).

Some believers are actually hollering because they can't pay their bills, but they just need to go to work! They're full of "super-faith," but with all their *hyper*-faith, they're starving to death!

You see, many believers don't seem to understand the difference between faith statements and foolishness. Some well-meaning believers have even entered into ridiculous financial contracts because they acted in presumption and folly.

I heard one person say, "Well, I'm going to put God on the line. Bless God, He's either going to meet my needs or else." And that person went out and signed a contract for a big automobile that he couldn't afford.

Of course, when it came time to pay for the car, he didn't have a penny. The car was repossessed, and then he said, "See, that faith business doesn't work! God's Word failed."

Situations like that can cause real confusion in the Body of Christ, especially for baby Christians who aren't mature enough in the Word to distinguish between faith and foolishness.

But that person had no business putting God on the line like that in the first place. Don't ever put God on the line! There's nowhere in the Bible where it says you can presumptuously say, "All right, God! You meet my need or else!"

God's Word does say we can put God in remembrance of His Word because He's already made certain provisions and promises for us (Isa. 43:26). But sometimes there's a fine line between boldly standing on the Word and getting arrogant with God.

It's the same way in sports. In basketball there's a distinction between playing a good hard game of basketball and playing dirty, illegal ball.

It's that way with faith. We need to be sure to play by the rules and principles set down for us in the Word. Even in faith, we need to stay right down the middle of the road based on the principles in God's Word.

Also, when you study the Word about faith, many times you'll find that you have to meet certain conditions before God can move on your behalf. For example, believers can't expect to live any way they want to and expect God to bless them with His abundance!

It disturbs me when believers make so-called "faith" statements supposedly based on the Word of God, but they don't have a lifestyle to match. They don't meet the conditions for God's blessing.

The Holy Spirit leads us into holiness and truth and upright living before God. When we meet God's conditions, *then* we reap a harvest of blessings from God.

I'm not saying I don't believe faith works. I've seen God move time and time again in answer to faith in His Word. But I didn't have to go around lying about it to get Him to move on my behalf either!

If I don't have any money and someone asks me if I have a financial need, I just say, "My God supplies all of my needs." I don't tell them that I don't have any money. But I declare God's Word by faith. However, if I said, "I have plenty of money," and I didn't have a cent, that would be a lie! Do you see the difference?

I know a Christian who was about to lose his building, his ministry, and everything else he had, but he just kept getting up in the pulpit Sunday after Sunday making what he thought were faith statements to his congregation.

He'd also made the same so-called faith statements to the unsaved people he bought his church from. He'd say, "Yes, the money is in the mail." But a month would pass, and he still hadn't mailed his mortgage payment.

Finally, litigation was brought against him, and it was a black spot against the man's ministry. Then a lot of people said, "See there, faith doesn't work. That proves faith confessions aren't scriptural."

But the man wasn't in faith at all! He was lying. He wasn't basing His faith on the Word. He wasn't even living up to the Word of God because he lied to his creditors. Therefore, God couldn't prosper him!

Put God in Remembrance of His Word

You see, a confession that's not based on the Word has no validity to it. It doesn't carry any weight in the court of Heaven! And many times if you ask believers what scriptures they're standing on, they don't have *any* scripture in their mouth *or* in their heart.

But that's not Bible faith. The Bible says we can put God in remembrance of His Word, and His Word will prosper in the situation (Isa. 55:11). When we plead our case before God our righteous Judge, we can expect Him to hear and answer our petitions.

Did you ever notice that when an attorney stands before a judge, he brings up past legal precedent? In other words, he pleads his case based on laws that have already been ruled on. He simply reminds the judge what the law already says. That is the legal way for an attorney to plead his case in a court of law.

That's exactly what your Heavenly Father wants you to do with Him.

Some people say, "You don't need to remind God of anything; He already knows everything!" But they must not have read Isaiah 43:26: *"Put me in remembrance: let us plead together: declare thou, that thou mayest be justified."* God invites us to remind Him of His Word.

When we remind God of His Word, we are just calling His attention to what He's already promised us. He said that because we're His children, our inheritance in Christ already belongs to us.

In the natural, children plead their case with their parents. Their parents make them a promise, and the children are quick to remind them of what they promised. Many times over the years, my children have put me in remembrance of what I've said!

That's all we're doing when we take the promises from the pages of God's Word and put Him in remembrance of what He said. In fact, God says in His Word that if earthly fathers know how to give good gifts to their children, how much more does He, our Heavenly Father, give good gifts to *His* children.

> **MATTHEW 7:11**
> **11 If ye then, being evil, know how to give good gifts unto your children, how much more shall your Father which is in heaven give good things to them that ask him?**

It pleases God when we study and meditate on His Word until it's down on the inside of us in our hearts, and then we bring it to His remembrance. That makes

Him want all the more to heap His abundant blessings upon us.

Line Up With God's Word!

Sometimes our problem is that we don't talk in line with God's Word. We say everything except what God says, and then we expect God to prosper what we're saying. But God can't prosper negative confessions filled with doubt, fear, half-truths, or out-and-out lies.

For example, many times God asks us to do something that seems impossible to us because He wants to show us the power in His Word. But when we say, "I can't!" and God says "You can!" then, really, we're calling God a liar.

Or in desperate circumstances, instead of saying, "God, why did this happen to me?" confess instead, "I don't know why this happened. But I am going to come out on the other side victorious because greater is He who is in me than he that is in the world! I am more than a conqueror through Christ who loves me."

Always talk in line with God's Word. For example, suppose you go to a doctor and he gives you a negative report. He's telling you the facts, all right. Recognize those facts, but then say, "Armed with the greater facts of God's Word, I say what God says: 'Himself bore my infirmities and carried my diseases. By His stripes I am healed!'"

In making faith confessions, some people think they're being scriptural when they deny that the problem exists. But you can't deny that the problem exists. That's not what faith is.

For example, if a doctor tells you that you've got a certain disease, then those are the facts based on *natural* circumstances. But that's not the last word on the matter. God's Word is the last word on the matter!

The facts of God's Word are higher than medical facts. God's Word contains *supernatural* facts. What does *God* say in His Word about your healing or your miracle? God's Word says He's already provided it for you at the Cross of Calvary!

ISAIAH 53:4,5
4 Surely he [Jesus] hath borne our griefs, and carried our sorrows: yet we did esteem him stricken, smitten of God, and afflicted.
5 But he was wounded for our transgressions, he was bruised for our iniquities: the chastisement of our peace was upon him; and with his stripes we are healed.

MATTHEW 8:17
17 That it might be fulfilled which was spoken by Esaias the prophet, saying, Himself took our infirmities, and bare our sicknesses.

1 PETER 2:24
24 Who his own self bare our sins in his own body on the tree, that we, being dead to sins, should live unto righteousness: by whose stripes ye were healed.

You see, facts are facts. Faith doesn't deny natural facts. Faith just looks at the higher facts of God's Word.

For example, if a woman is pregnant, that's a fact. If she went to the doctor and he confirmed that she was pregnant, it doesn't matter how much she tries to deny it, the evidence is still there in her body — she's going to have a baby!

If you're sick, there's no use trying to deny that you are sick. That's a fact. And usually when you're sick, everybody else can see that you don't feel well. But to be in faith, you don't have to deny those natural facts. Just be armed in your spirit with the greater facts of God's Word.

Let me tell you what faith is in a practical way so we can understand it. It's just looking at what *God* said, not at circumstances or anything else.

In other words, to succeed in God, you've got to quit looking at all the measly, insignificant natural facts that try to tell you God's Word isn't true and that believing God's Word doesn't work. Natural, circumstantial facts exist, but they aren't greater than the fact of who God is!

God is more than enough to meet any need, and by His great power, He can come down and change natural facts and circumstances. His power on the scene brings health and healing. His power on the scene brings your miracle and abundantly meets your needs, whatever it is.

You see, our problem is that sometimes we stop looking at what God has said and done in our lives, and instead we look *only* at the natural facts — the circumstances. So many times that's what causes us to get out of faith.

It's up to each one of us to look at what God's Word promises, so the Word can begin to override our natural circumstances. Get ahold of the promises of God! Make faith confessions in line with God's Word so you can possess your promised land.

Confession Works in Salvation

Remember, it was Jesus Himself who talked about the God-kind of faith of believing and confessing God's Word! Actually, God's inevitable law of faith works for salvation too.

Yes, the same principles of faith so many people want to quarrel about are used by every person who gets saved. You can't even get saved without faith and confession!

> **ROMANS 10:9,10**
> 9   That if thou shalt CONFESS WITH THY MOUTH the Lord Jesus, and shalt BELIEVE IN THINE HEART that God hath raised him from the dead, thou shalt be saved.
> 10 For with THE HEART MAN BELIEVETH unto righteousness; and with THE MOUTH CONFESSION IS MADE unto SALVATION.

Romans 10:9,10 contains the same principle as Mark 11:23,24. You *believe* God's Word in your heart, you *confess* it with your mouth, and you *receive* your salvation.

What do you believe and confess? That Jesus Christ is your Lord. You confess that God raised Jesus from the dead and you receive Jesus as the Savior of your sins. When you believe and confess that Jesus Christ is your Savior and Lord, you are saved or born again.

The Benefits of Your Salvation

PSALM 103:2
2   Bless the Lord, O my soul, and forget not ALL HIS BENEFITS.

The same principles of believing in your heart and confessing with your mouth that brought you into salvation will also help you receive any other benefit from God, including your full inheritance in Christ.

As you learn how God's principles of Bible faith work, then you can begin to exercise your faith to receive every provision that belongs to you in God's Word. For example, once you learn how faith works, you can begin to use your faith for souls to come into the Kingdom of God!

Every person who believes in his heart and confesses with his mouth that Jesus Christ is Lord is a child of God. Maybe he's never used the principles of the God-kind of faith to receive the other benefits that belong to him from God's storehouse of riches, but he's still a child of God.

We shouldn't criticize those who don't believe in receiving all the benefits of their redemption, such as healing and prosperity. They'll still go to Heaven; they'll just miss out on God's best down here.

As long as you've acted on Romans 10:9,10, you are

a part of the Body of Christ. That's true whether or not you ever receive all of God's manifold blessings that are freely offered to you as part of your inheritance in Christ. I call those blessings the *fringe benefits* of our redemption.

Probably all of us at one time or another have worked at a job that offered certain fringe benefits. When the company hired you, they probably explained the fringe benefits that were available to you. You could enjoy those benefits at any time because they belonged to you as an employee of that company.

But no employer is going to force you to take advantage of the fringe benefits his company offers! For example, an employer won't demand that you go to the doctor or to the dentist, even though it may be a benefit that rightfully belongs to you.

God has given us all the wonderful benefits of our redemption through Jesus Christ. Those benefits are part of our redemption, but God won't push them off on us, just like a company won't push its benefits off on an employee.

It's up to *us* to take advantage of what belongs to us! The way to receive our benefits in Christ is through faith in what God has already said in His Word.

Faith is really a very simple spiritual law. First, we study the Word to find out what our benefits include. Then we believe God's Word in our heart for those provisions and speak the Word about them. That's how we appropriate by faith what belongs to us.

Faith is produced when our heart and our words

line up with God's Word. Then as we walk in obedience
to God, everything God has promised us will come to
pass in our lives. That's the way God has provided for
each one of us to enter into our promised land. That's
the *God-kind* of faith.

Speak to Your Mountain!

Some people want to quarrel with Mark 11:23,24,
even though *Jesus* said it — not man! Actually, in Mark
11:23, Jesus talked about two faith principles. First, He
talked about making *faith confessions* based on God's
Word so a person can "*. . . have whatsoever he saith.*"

Second, Jesus talked about speaking to your mountain. Speaking to your mountain activates the God-kind
of faith.

> **MARK 11:23,24**
> **23 For verily I say unto you, That whosoever shall
> SAY UNTO THIS MOUNTAIN, Be thou removed,
> and be thou cast into the sea; and shall not
> DOUBT in his heart, but shall believe that those
> things which he SAITH shall come to pass; he shall
> have whatsoever he SAITH.**
> **24 Therefore I say unto you, What things soever
> ye desire, when ye pray, believe that ye receive
> them, and ye shall have them.**

Jesus said, "*Whosoever shall SAY UNTO THIS
MOUNTAIN, Be thou removed, and be thou cast into
the sea . . . he shall have whatsoever he saith.*"

Jesus is telling us in verse 23 to *confess* God's Word

and to *speak* to the mountains in our lives. Mountains are insurmountable obstacles or hindrances that Satan has erected to keep us from possessing all that God has for us in this life. Each one of us has insurmountable mountains that we can't get over or go around by ourselves.

God tells us in Mark 11:23 what to do about those mountains. He said *we* are supposed to *speak* to them! What are we supposed to speak? We're supposed to speak God's Word to those mountains so we can go on and possess everything God has for us in life.

Identify Your Mountain of Hindrance

But before you can speak God's Word to your mountain or problem, you've got to identify what the problem is. Find out what the mountain of hindrance really is that's keeping you from your promised land — all that you desire in God.

Sometimes the reason believers don't receive answers to their prayers is that they've never identified and isolated the source of their problem. They really don't know what it is that is hindering them in life, so they don't pray specifically.

Think what would happen if you tried to fix your car the same way some believers try to solve their problems.

For example, if the engine in your car isn't running properly, you could just start working on the car, saying, "The engine isn't running right, so I'll rebuild the carburetor." But if the engine isn't running right and you rebuild the carburetor, you're still going to have engine problems.

Or you could say, "Well, I'll just change the spark plugs." You can go through that car rebuilding everything but the engine, and you'll still have problems.

But if you don't want to spend a lot of money, you'd better identify the problem before you start working on anything else. You just don't start fixing things, hoping that something you do will cure the problem. First you identify the problem and fix that.

Too many mechanics spend a customer's money, and they never identify the problem! But if they're going to do the job correctly, they'll have to identify the source of the problem and take care of it by replacing the defective part. There's no use replacing parts that are working properly.

It's the same way in our Christian walk. There's no use praying hours in generalities when we've got a specific problem we can't solve. If we don't know what's causing the hindrance, we need to pray and ask God to identify the source of the problem for us.

Of course, you may be communing with God when you pray in generalities, and that's fine. But if you'd pray specifically about the problem you're facing, God would answer you specifically.

You'd get far more accomplished if you'd ask God to show you exactly what your mountain of hindrance really is. Then you could deal with it scripturally.

What's Your Mountain?

What mountain stands between you and possessing everything God has for you in life? Whatever your mountain is, ask God to help you identify it. For example, is your mountain fear? Maybe your mountain is a financial need, sickness, confusion, strife, or marriage problems. Maybe it's jealousy, resentment, lack of freedom in prayer, or even thoughts of suicide.

Yes, some believers can get so caught up in hopelessness as they face the problems of life that they want to commit suicide. Christians don't usually want to talk about that, but suicide is a major problem in this country today.

But we in the Body of Christ can help those people — if they will allow us to. People can be taught how to get out of that pit of despair so they can lead fulfilled, productive lives.

Bitterness and self-pity can be huge mountains standing between you and your promised land. Many believers have trouble with self-pity; they're always having pity parties. That can be a real mountain in their lives because it keeps them from progressing spiritually.

Self-pity — the poor-ole-me attitude — leads to depression and frustration. Then those negative feelings lead to utter helplessness and hopelessness, and it gives the devil a playground in your life.

Once you open the door to the devil through self-pity, you allow him to whisper to you: "You can get out of this mess real easy. Just stop your life right now. You'll get out of the problem, and you'll have no more worries."

And sad to say, a few Christians do get to the point where they think about ending their own life. But that wouldn't happen to Christian people if they really knew and acted on their rights and privileges in Christ.

Maybe the mountain in your life is grumbling and complaining. Maybe every time anyone says something to you that you don't like, you start grumbling. My wife used to say certain things to me, and sometimes I would grumble about it. The main reason I grumbled was that I knew she was right!

I'd do what she asked me to do, but I'd just walk off grumbling. If you are married maybe you can identify with that. Sometimes wives have a way of being right, and many times their husbands don't want to admit it.

The more spiritually immature we are, the more we grumble. When we get a little more wisdom, we start to realize that grumbling isn't doing anyone any good — including ourselves — so we start trying to change some of those negative traits.

But without thinking, we can carry these same negative natural traits over into our spiritual walk with God. If God says something to us that we don't particularly like, we start grumbling, "Well, Lord, I just don't understand . . . grumble, grumble, grumble."

As long as the Lord wants us to do something we *want* to do, we get excited about it, "Whoo! Praise the Lord! Glory! Let me at it, Lord!" But if it's something we don't want to do, we complain, "Now, Lord, let's talk about this a minute . . ."

You may feel like you have a mountain of stubbornness. Of course, none of us have ever thought we were stubborn — it's just our wife or husband or our mamma or daddy who's stubborn!

Or sometimes people blame their stubborn streak on their heritage, and say, "Oh, that's just my Irish nature," or "I got my temper from my father's side of the family." It's human nature to always want to put the blame on someone or something else.

But we can't blame our negative traits on our heritage. That just creates a bigger mountain, because then we never deal with the problem. Actually, it's our flesh nature that we need to deal with! And sometimes we're *allowing* the devil to dominate us!

We need to realize that stubbornness leads to rebellion. And the Bible says that rebellion is like the sin of witchcraft (1 Sam. 15:22,23). We'd better be careful about stubbornness and rebellion in our lives!

Every person has their own insurmountable mountains in life. We each have our own personalities and different mountains that have tried to hinder us spiritually from possessing our promised land. What affects one person may not affect another person. What's a stumbling block to you, may not be a stumbling block to me.

But it shows real spiritual growth when we get on the other side of one of those mountains! We've probably all looked back on our lives and wondered, *Why in the world did I ever let* that *give me a problem?* Isn't it wonderful that with God nothing is impossible! He continually helps us grow and overcome insurmountable objects.

As we grow with God and we grow in grace, we outgrow problems that were once insurmountable mountains to us. But as we overcome one mountain, we're usually confronted with another mountain — a new challenge to face in life. Each time we're confronted with a new mountain, we have to grow in God to bring that mountain down to the size of a molehill!

And with every new problem, we need to identify what is really causing us the problem. Once we identify the source of the problem, that is only the beginning. Then we're ready to do something to correct the problem.

That's where speaking to the mountain comes in. Speaking God's Word to bring your mountains down is one way God has given us to overcome our problems and claim our promised land.

Be Bold!

You'll have to be bold to speak to your mountain. You don't accomplish anything by meekly trying to speak to a problem that's hindering your progress. You've got to speak to it with authority in Jesus' Name. And you've got to speak the *Word* of God to it, because the Word is the only thing that has the ability to make it a molehill!

What gives us boldness and authority to speak to our mountain? Finding out what the Word of God says about who we are in Christ. In other words, we must find out what our authority is as believers.

Once you understand your authority in Christ, then you need to begin to act on the words of Jesus. Notice that in Mark 11:23, it does not say we are to pray *to* the mountain or pray *against* the mountain.

Mark 11:24 is talking about praying: *"Therefore I say unto you, What things soever ye desire, WHEN YE PRAY, believe that ye receive them, and ye shall have them."*

You have to believe you receive your answer from God by faith *before* you see the answer manifested. But Mark 11:23 is talking about making faith confessions and speaking to your mountain.

I've heard a lot of people pray, "Lord, I'm praying against this hindrance in my life." No, you *pray* to the *Lord*, but you *speak* to your *mountain* with authority using God's Word.

You can pray to the Father like this:

> I thank You, Father, that You've given me the authority through the Word of God and by the shed blood of the Lord Jesus Christ to speak to the problems in my life that have stood in my way like a mountain of hindrance.
>
> Therefore, based on Your Word, I take my authority in Jesus' Name and I speak to this problem according to Your Word.

Then quote the Word at your mountain! Don't *pray* to the mountain! *Speak* to the mountain!

So many times believers pray, "Oh God! O-o-oh God! O-o-o-o-h God! Take the mountain away, Lord! Move the mountain, Lord!" But you're wasting your time and the

Lord's time if you're just praying about your mountain instead of speaking to it. The Lord has given you the authority to speak to whatever is standing in your way.

God has given you a way of escape by telling you to speak to the problem. You speak to your mountain in the Name of Jesus, because Jesus has already won the victory over any mountain you will ever face in life.

It doesn't matter what problems you face in life, Jesus Christ has already triumphed over them. That's why you don't need to cry and beg and plead and fast for God to remove the problem. Just speak to it with authority based on the Word of God, because the Word has already triumphed over it!

Now don't go off and say that I said we're not supposed to pray and fast. I didn't say that at all. Prayer and fasting have their place. But we need to learn when a situation calls for praying and fasting and when it calls for standing in our place of authority to overcome the problem.

You need to realize the authority you possess based on Jesus' triumph over the devil. Your circumstance is nothing for the Word to move out of the way!

You won't be able to speak to your problem with authority if you have doubt in your heart. Remember, Mark 11:23 said, *"Whosoever shall say unto this mountain . . . and SHALL NOT DOUBT in his heart . . . he shall have whatsoever he saith."*

You can't doubt in your heart and confess something with your mouth and expect what you confess to come to pass.

What are doubt and unbelief? Actually, doubt is not committing yourself wholeheartedly to the Word of God. You see, when you commit yourself to something, you have complete faith in it.

For example, when you sit down in a chair, you've got faith that the chair will hold you up. You've committed your body to that chair in faith that the chair won't break under your weight.

Once my wife and I went to my mother-in-law's house to visit, and I sat down in one of her chairs. As I leaned back, the whole back of the chair fell off, and I almost ended up on the floor! The next time we visited her home, she said to me, "Ken, I bought you a chair you can't break!"

If I doubt that a chair will hold up under the weight of my body, I have no faith in it, and I'm not going to sit in it. But if I'm sure a chair is sturdy, I wouldn't think a thing about resting my whole weight on it.

In the past I've sat down in some chairs I didn't trust, so I just barely put my whole weight on it. It's a strain to sit in a chair you think is going to break at any minute.

But the point is, when most of us sit down in a chair, we believe that chair will hold us up. So we trust it, and we don't waiver in faith about sitting there.

Real faith in God is like that. It believes and doesn't waiver. Real faith commits to what God says and never turns away from that.

If you're in faith, you never turn back from what *God* says. You never wonder if His promises are going to work. You just trust in the Lord that He will perform what He said He would perform.

Real faith believes the Word. For example, real faith walks over, sits down, and abides on the promises of God's Word, trusting that they work because they're God's Word. Real faith possesses every promise of God and knows that His Word will hold up under the pressures and strains of life's circumstances.

Real faith also speaks God's Word to the mountains that obscure the view to our promised land. Real faith believes that God's Word works and doesn't doubt that what it speaks will come to pass.

Real faith says, "Father, I believe that as I'm faithful to speak Your Word over the situation, Your Word is at work removing my mountains."

Sit down and occupy all the promises of God's Word. Claim them and take ahold of them! Make them yours in every difficult situation. The Word will hold you up! It won't fail you or let you down because God's Word never returns to Him void. It accomplishes what it was sent to do (Isa. 55:11).

However, if you keep talking about the mountains that loom up before you, they will get bigger and bigger. If you keep confessing, "I've got so many problems, I just don't know what to do!" your problems will only get bigger and bigger. And sad to say, God will get smaller and smaller *to you*.

Have you ever noticed that when people start talking or gossiping about a little problem, all of a sudden it becomes a giant problem that's all out of proportion. By

the time people get done talking about the problem —
it's the size of a mountain! It's amazing that it started
out just as a little molehill to begin with!

I remember when I was in school, one day a fellow
drove out of the parking lot too fast and his car slid
sideways before he could get it back under control.
Someone saw that incident and started telling everyone
that the fellow had a wreck.

By the time it got around the school, that little incident had turned into a bad wreck. People were saying,
"Man, he slid his car sideways, rolled over, and was hit
by a semi-truck!" Really, nothing had happened, but the
more people talked about it, the worse it got.

Your mountains are the same way. The more you talk
about them, the worse they get. The more you talk about
your impossibilities, the higher you build them in your
own sight until they tower in the sky in front of you.

But instead of talking about your mountain, speak
to it with the authority in God's Word. Then don't talk
about it anymore, except to speak the Word of God at it.
The Word says if we would use the Word of God on our
mountains and believe in our hearts what we say, we'd
receive our answer.

Someone says, "Oh, I tried that, but nothing happened." The Word of God doesn't say anything about
you *trying* to make something come to pass. It just said
if you speak God's Word over your circumstance and
you believe it in your heart, God's Word will perform
what it was sent to accomplish.

Hold fast to your confession! Hold on to your profession of faith (Heb. 10:23). Don't let loose of your faith confession.

Use the Word of God on that mountain until you've whittled it down to a molehill! Then you can cross over the top of it and go on and do what God's called you to do.

And once you get that mountain whittled down to size, if it ever tries to overshadow you again, just recognize it doesn't have to affect you anymore.

Stand on your confession: "That mountain is not a part of my life anymore. It does not have any influence over me, and I will not succumb to it any longer because the Word of God says I've been delivered and set free."

But you need to understand that when you go out and start removing the mountains in your life, it's a big job. Mountains don't always get moved overnight. Sometimes it takes time to move those things out of your way that have been there for so long.

The same is true in the natural realm. Have you ever watched a road crew remove a mountain so they can put in a road? It's a big job. It doesn't happen overnight. Sometimes it takes days and weeks of blasting to bring that mountain down to size.

I remember when I was a child, my family and I traveled with Dad back and forth to California holding meetings. This was before all the interstate highways, and we always used to drive on the old Route 66.

I remember seeing those road construction crews out there blasting their way through the sides of mountains. They literally just blew up a mountain, piece by piece.

All the traffic was stopped on that stretch of the road, and we had to turn off all our radios and our two-way equipment because the road crew was getting ready to blast. They'd drilled into the mountainside and they were just getting ready to set off the charges.

Once they pushed the button on that detonator, you could see rocks flying everywhere. It looked like a volcano going off. Some of the small fragments even came sailing down on top of the cars that were parked quite a distance from the mountain.

Then the workmen would go back to the mountain site, clean up the rocks and debris, start drilling again, and pack the mountain with dynamite again. Then they'd set off another blast, and it would cause that mountain to crumble some more.

And after a few days, they had blasted out of their way what had seemed to be an impenetrable mountain. What was once a mountain of hindrance was reduced to flat land, and the road crew could start laying a roadbed.

It's the same way in the spiritual realm. When you speak God's Word in faith, you're setting off a detonator of a powerful blast that is demolishing your mountain piece by piece. That's why you can't give up after quoting the Word a few times.

As you faithfully quote the Word, give the Word time to work on the problem. Many times those mountains in your life are not going to leave overnight. But if you'll keep your confidence in God's Word and diligently speak it over your problems, they *will* leave.

Do you have a mountain or a problem in your life you want to move out of the way? That's doesn't mean you're not a Christian or that you lack faith. You've just got a barrier that's standing in the way of receiving your promised land.

If you've got insurmountable mountains in your life, write them down on a piece of paper. Identify them. Be specific with God. Write them down so you know exactly what has to be blasted out of your life.

Then stay in faith by saying, "I've prayed in faith, so I believe I've received my petition according to the Word of God. Now I'm going to speak to this hindrance — this mountain — in the Name of Jesus and I tell it to be removed and be cast into the sea. I believe as I speak God's Word over my situation that this mountain is moving out of my life."

Then from a heart of faith in God's Word, make this confession:

> Heavenly Father, I thank You that the Word of God declares that I have the authority to speak to the mountains in my life. Therefore, I exercise my rights and privileges based on Mark 11:23.
>
> Father, Your Son Jesus said that if I would speak to the mountain that is hindering me and not doubt in my heart, then I would receive my answer and that mountain would be removed. Therefore, in Jesus' Name I command these mountains to be removed!
>
> So based on Your Word, I hold up before You the

mountain that has blocked my path from receiving what You have for me. It is _____ [name your mountain]. I take authority over that mountain, and I speak to it. Be removed in the Name of Jesus!

I thank You, Lord, that as I speak Your Word over this mountain of hindrance, Your Word will begin moving this problem out of my way!

I thank You, Lord, that I will no longer be under the shadow of this problem in my life. No longer will that mountain hinder the sun and the blessings of God from shining in my life.

When you're confronted with an impossible mountain or problem in your life, begin to look at that impossibility through the eyes of God's Word. And then watch the scenery change! Those mountains you thought were so impossible to cross will all of a sudden look just like little molehills.

As you're faithful to speak God's Word over your situation, those road blocks that were impossible to traverse will suddenly become nothing but stepping-stones to the victory on the other side. Then you can boldly walk in to your promised land and claim all that belongs to you in Christ!

Chapter 2

The Law of Faith
In the Old Testament

Many people teach that the promises of God are not for us today. They claim that the principles of confession are not biblical because we only find them in the New Testament.

They say, "A New Testament truth must be established in the Old Testament, too, because everything in the New Testament has its beginning in the Old Testament."

But God's inevitable law of faith — confessing God's Word and receiving what you say — is a principle that was also established in the Old Testament. I can show you that the Israelites confessed what they believed in their heart, and they got exactly what they said.

The passages in Numbers chapters 13 and 14 recount the Israelites' journey into the Promised Land. The Israelites' confession as they tried to enter their Promised land is a perfect example of Mark 11:23 in action. The children of Israel give us a biblical example of people who received exactly what they confessed.

The Israelites had the opportunity to take God at His Word and continually confess their faith in Him. If they had just believed God and acted on their faith by using faith-filled words, they could have entered their Promised Land. Instead, they confessed defeat — and that's exactly what they got.

In the New Testament, the Apostle Paul wrote that everything the children of Israel experienced happened as ensamples or examples for us (1 Cor. 10:11). So we can learn from their mistakes. We can see how disobedience to God kept them from receiving their Promised Land.

The Israelites had been in bondage in Egypt for 430 years. Egypt is a type of sin and bondage. Therefore, coming out of Egypt's bondage is a type of coming out of sin. Even in the Old Testament, God delivered His people out of sin and bondage!

Not only did God deliver His people out of sin and bondage, but through many signs and wonders, He supernaturally brought them into a land of milk and honey — their Promised Land!

> **EXODUS 3:7,8**
> 7   And the Lord said, I have surely seen the afflic-
> tion of my people which are in Egypt, and have
> heard their cry by reason of their taskmasters; for
> I know their sorrows;
> 8   And I am come down to deliver them out of the
> hand of the Egyptians, and to bring them up out of
> that land UNTO A GOOD LAND AND A LARGE,
> UNTO A LAND FLOWING WITH MILK AND
> HONEY; unto the place of the Canaanites, and the
> Hittites, and the Amorites, and the Perizzites, and
> the Hivites, and the Jebusites.

Under the New Covenant, God has done the same thing for us, His people. He's given us an inheritance in Christ, which is exceedingly abundantly above all that we could ask or think (Eph. 3:20).

Some people think that the Canaan Land of the Old Testament is a type of Heaven, but it's not. Canaan couldn't be a type of Heaven because there aren't any giants to fight in Heaven.

For the New Testament believer, Canaan Land is a type of our Christian walk down here on this earth. Canaan is a type of entering into our promised land by receiving our inheritance in Christ while we live on this earth.

We know that Canaan Land is a type of our Christian walk on this earth because there aren't any battles to fight or struggles to overcome in Heaven.

In the Christian walk down here, you do have some trials, some struggles, and some attacks of the enemy. Yes, you'll have to go in and overcome the giants that stand between you and what belongs to you in Christ.

You'll have to crucify the flesh and tear down some walls and barriers that the enemy will try to erect. The enemy will try to come in and set up camp, and you'll have to go in and get him out.

And sometimes like the Israelites did at the town of Ai (Joshua 7:1-26), you'll have to stop and find out if you're being hindered in your spiritual walk because of sin and disobedience. When you deal with sin in your life, then things will start working out right again for you.

But even though there are obstacles to overcome and giants to bring subject to Jesus' Name, God still expects us to go in and possess what rightfully belongs to us in Christ. We do that by claiming the promises in

God's Word and by walking in obedience to His perfect
will. Then God will help us possess what belongs to us
through our redemption in Christ.

God helped the Israelites possess their Promised
Land too. God raised up Moses and sent him to deliver
His people out of Egypt by miraculous signs and won-
ders.

The Israelites came out of Egypt's sin and bondage
and traveled across the wilderness of Paran until they
finally arrived at Kadesh Barnea. They looked across
the River Jordan and beheld the land that God said
belonged to them.

God told Moses that He was giving them the land of
Canaan as their possession. He said it was a land that
flowed with milk and honey, and it was their own
promised possession to dwell in (Exod. 3:8,17).

> **DEUTERONOMY 1:8**
> 8   Behold, I have set the land before you: go in
> and **POSSESS THE LAND** which the Lord sware
> unto your fathers, Abraham, Isaac, and Jacob, to
> give unto them and to their seed after them.

God said, "I've given you the land; it's yours. But
now *you* go over and possess it." That's also what God
says about all His promises to us today: "They're
yours — now *you* go possess them."

I don't know about you, but I want to do more than
just look at the pages of the Bible and read the words
and see the promises. Some people read the words of
the Bible, and they see all the great things God does for

others, but they're not possessing the blessings of God for themselves.

I'm determined to possess the blessings of God for myself because they belong to me! God has given them to me in Christ. All the blessings of God are part of my rightful inheritance in Christ. And they're part of *your* rightful inheritance in Christ too.

Look at it this way. Can God fully perform what He's said He would? Can He still save and heal? Can He still baptize with the Holy Spirit? Can He still deliver? Yes! Yes, He can! He can still abundantly bless His people.

But in order for each one of us to enter our own promised land, we'll have to believe the Word. We'll have to believe that God sent His Word and healed us. We'll have to believe that by Jesus' stripes we are healed and set free. And we'll have to believe that whosoever is born of God overcomes the world.

When you're fully persuaded that what God has promised, He will perform, then you're on the path to enter your promised land. When you believe that and confess it and walk in obedience to God, that's when you'll begin possessing what belongs to you in Christ.

Remind yourself daily that you're going to receive from God, and appropriate what belongs to you. Remind yourself that God has already bought and paid for your inheritance in Christ and that He's promised it to you. Then receive it for yourself, and believe that God will do what He promised!

God Always Has a Plan
For Possessing the Land!

In the Old Testament, God promised the Israelites
that He would bring them into their Promised Land.
But how were the Israelites supposed to possess the
land? God gave Moses a plan. God will always give His
children a plan, showing them exactly how to possess
what He has promised them.

First, God told Moses to send twelve men who were
the heads of the tribes of the people into Canaan to spy
out the land.

> **NUMBERS 13:1-3,16,17**
> 1   And the Lord spake unto Moses, saying,
> 2   SEND THOU MEN, THAT THEY MAY SEARCH
> THE LAND OF CANAAN, which I give unto the
> children of Israel: of every tribe of their fathers
> shall ye send a man, every one a ruler among
> them.
> 3   And Moses by the commandment of the Lord
> sent them from the wilderness of Paran: all those
> men were heads of the children of Israel....
> 16 These are the names of the men which Moses
> SENT TO SPY OUT THE LAND....
> 17 And Moses SENT THEM TO SPY OUT THE
> LAND OF CANAAN, and said unto them, Get you
> up this way southward, and go up into the moun-
> tain.

Those of you who have been in the armed forces of
your country know about reconnaissance teams. A
reconnaissance team is the first of the troops to go into
enemy territory to spy on the enemy. The reconnais-

sance team doesn't engage the enemy in fire; their mission is to chart a map showing where the enemy's machine gun or cannon placements are hidden.

It's the job of the reconnaissance team to return to their company unobserved by the enemy and report on the enemy's whereabouts and artillery. Then an offensive attack can be mounted against the opposing forces.

NUMBERS 13:26,27
26 And they [the Israelites spies] **went and came to Moses, and to Aaron, and to all the congregation of the children of Israel, unto the wilderness of Paran, to Kadesh; and brought back word unto them, and unto all the congregation, and shewed them the fruit of the land.**
27 And they told him, and said, We came unto the land wither thou sentest us, and SURELY IT FLOWETH WITH MILK AND HONEY; and THIS IS THE FRUIT OF IT.

In verse 26, the spies had gone into the land and returned with their report to Moses and the people. A good reconnaissance team immediately reports their findings to the commander, so he can plan their next strategy.

So the twelve spies reported back to Moses and Aaron. Moses was the commander in chief and Aaron the priest was his aide. The Israelite spies showed the people the abundance of fruit in the land and told them that the land "flowed with milk and honey" (v. 27).

Notice in verse 27 that when the spies came back from spying out the land, first they started out agreeing with what God had told them about the land. They said it was a land flowing with milk and honey.

The spies even brought back some of the fruit, and said, "It's a good land. It has everything we need! We've been wandering out in this awful barren wilderness, but this land God wants to give us is plentiful in crops and water. And besides all that — it's beautiful. And look at the fruit that grows there. It's huge!"

But then ten of the spies made a fatal mistake. They gave the Israelites an evil report of the land, which was contrary to what God had told them. They opposed God with their words.

NUMBERS 13:28-33
28 NEVERTHELESS the people be strong that dwell in the land, and the cities are walled, and very great: and moreover we saw the children of Anak there.
29 The Amalekites dwell in the land of the south: and the Hittites, and the Jebusites, and the Amorites, dwell in the mountains: and the Canaanites dwell by the sea, and by the coast of Jordan.
30 And Caleb stilled the people before Moses, and said, Let us go up at once, and possess it; for we are well able to overcome it.
31 But the men that went up with him said, We be not able to go up against the people; for they are stronger than we.
32 And they brought up AN EVIL REPORT of the land which they had searched unto the children of Israel, saying, The land, through which we have gone to search it, is a land that eateth up the inhabitants thereof; and all the people that we saw in it are men of a great stature.
33 And there we saw the giants, the sons of Anak,

which come of the giants: and we were in our own sight as grasshoppers, and so we were in their sight.

Look at verse 28. In the English language, when you see a "nevertheless" connected to a positive statement, you immediately know a negative statement is about to follow. People usually tell the good report first, and then the bad report.

So first the ten spies talked about all the good things in the land (v. 27). But then they began to talk about the giants in the land, and you can almost hear their voices drop to a whisper in fear: *"NEVERTHE-LESS the people be strong that dwell in the land, and the cities are walled, and very great . . ."* (v. 28).

So the ten spies were really saying, "We saw the land God gave us, and it was just exactly like He said it would be. It was a land flowing with milk and honey. We know that God said we could take the land, *but* the people are too strong for us. The cities are walled and very great, and there are giants in the land!"

What did God call the Israelites' doubt and unbelief? He called it an *evil report* because it contradicted what He had already told them. A report of doubt and unbelief is an evil report. Why? Because doubt and unbelief contradict the Word of God.

The ten Israelite spies contradicted what God had told them! God told them to possess the land. God doesn't look at circumstances and say, "It's impossible." God looks in faith at what *He* can do in the midst of impossible circumstances!

You need to realize that anything God has promised you in His Word already belongs to you. All of God's blessings and benefits are part of your promised land.

But the devil will try to keep you from possessing what is yours. You must talk in line with God's Word to receive what God has for you, and you must possess it by faith.

When the devil tries to steal your God-given possessions, are you going to let him? In the natural, would you let someone walk into your home and steal your possessions? No, you wouldn't!

For example, if someone came along and hooked your car up to the back of his bumper and started pulling it away, would you just sit there and let him?

Would you just meekly say, "Well, I thought that car was mine, but I guess it's not"? No, you wouldn't! You'd get up and go after it and take possession of what belongs to you.

Then why do we stand back when the devil tries to steal from us? We whine, "I thought the Lord was going to give me my miracle, but I guess He isn't." What we need to do is rise up in faith and take possession of what belongs to us according to God's Word.

An evil report can not only hurt your faith, but it can also affect the people around you. The ten spies not only contradicted God and hindered their own faith, but their evil report got the other Israelites in an uproar.

We know the people were upset, because in verse 30 it says that Caleb had to still the people and get them quiet again before he could even talk!

In other words, the people were talking so loudly among themselves that Caleb had to get up and say, "Would you people please be quiet and listen to what I have to say!" That finally got their attention.

Then full of conviction, Caleb said, ". . . *Let us go up at once, and possess it; for WE ARE WELL ABLE TO OVERCOME IT*" (v. 30). Caleb was speaking in faith. He agreed with God. He had the God-kind of faith Jesus talked about in Mark 11:23 and 24. He confessed what he believed in his heart based on what *God* had said.

Caleb was really saying, "Let's go up at once and take what is ours! Let's receive what God has given us, for with God's help, we are well able to do the job He's set before us!"

But the ten spies spoke what was in their hearts — doubt and unbelief. Look at the lack of faith in their statement: ". . . *We be NOT able to go up against the people; for they are stronger than we*" (v. 31). What a negative confession!

God never told the Israelites that they had to be stronger than the giants in that land. God is stronger, and that's all that mattered! After all, God was the One fighting the Israelites' battles for them. Therefore, the Israelites were really speaking against God by showing their lack of faith in *Him*.

The Israelites were really saying to Caleb, "Caleb, what's the matter with you? You know we can't go up against those people. They're stronger and better equipped than we are."

The ten spies didn't agree with God. With their words, they built such an atmosphere of doubt and unbelief among the people, you could cut it with a knife!

Didn't they remember all the signs and wonders God had performed for them when He brought them out of Egypt and supernaturally sustained them in the wilderness?

Think about it. God had already told the Israelites that *He* had given them the land. All they had to do was possess it. God was the One who would enable them to fulfill His command. So the ten spies were really saying, "Yes, God said He gave us the land, but He can't do what He said He would!"

You see, once you allow yourself to get into a state of depression, your thinking will be wrong, and then your talking will be wrong. Once you start talking wrong and believing wrong, you'll contradict something God has told you, *and* you'll contradict His promise to you. You'll even contradict your own confessions of faith, all because your thinking isn't in agreement with God.

That's exactly what the Israelites did. And their evil report got even worse. Remember they said it was a great land, but as they got more and more negative, they contradicted themselves and said it was a land that devoured the inhabitants: *"The land . . . is a land that eateth up the inhabitants thereof"* (v. 32).

Now keep in mind that these ten men went into the land of Canaan as spies. In other words, they didn't let the people in the land see them because the Israelites were working as undercover agents for the Israelite army. But notice what the Israelites spies said in the very next verse.

NUMBERS 13:32,33
32 . . . all the people we saw in it are men of a great stature.
33 And there we saw the giants, the sons of Anak, which come of the giants: and we were in our own sight as grasshoppers, and SO WE WERE IN THEIR SIGHT.

The spies said, "We saw the giants, and in our own sight, we were like grasshoppers." That statement was true. After seeing those giants, I'm sure the Israelites did feel like grasshoppers! But did they forget that they had an Almighty God who had delivered them with great signs and wonders from the land of Egypt?

Their next statement was inspired by the devil. It was full of doubt, unbelief, and fear. They said, "We were as grasshoppers in the giants' sight too!"

But how did the Israelites know the giants thought of them as grasshoppers? Remember, the giants never saw the Israelites because the Hebrews went into the land undercover as spies. So the Israelites statement didn't make any sense because the giants didn't even see them!

If you went on a dangerous mission as a spy, you sure wouldn't let the enemy see you and know what you're doing, would you? No, you'd stay undercover. So those ten spies were just *presuming* what the giants were thinking. They were actually thinking the worst and putting words in the giants' mouths.

The real truth of the matter was that the Israelites saw *themselves* as grasshoppers, so they thought every-one else did too! How many times have we Christians done the same thing!

Instead of calling themselves grasshoppers, the Israelites should have said, "We are victorious because of God's promise to us. We are more than conquerors. Those giants are grasshoppers *in our sight!*"

To successfully receive everything that God has for you in this life, you've got to say what God says: "I am more than a conqueror through Christ who loves me. I am a victor, because greater is He that is in me, than he that is in the world. *Nothing* is impossible with God!"

Either you have a big God and a little devil, or you have a big devil and a little God. And when you think of yourself as a weak, puny little grasshopper, you're in doubt and unbelief just like the children of Israel. If you think of yourself as a grasshopper, then your God is too small.

Another kind of doubt and unbelief is found in the statement, "I can't." How many times have you said, "I can't"? Realize that anytime you say that, you're talking doubt and unbelief because the Bible says you *can* do all things through Christ who strengthens you (Phil. 4:13).

So don't ever say you *can't* do something. No, you won't always have the ability in yourself, but God does! If you don't think you have the ability to do something, go to God and He'll give you the ability. It's God's promise to you that you can do *all* things through Christ who strengthens you.

Maybe you've told God you can't do something because you think you lack wisdom. But the Bible says, *"If any of you lack wisdom, let him ask of God, that GIVETH to all men LIBERALLY, and upbraideth not; and it shall be given him"* (James 1:5).

In other words, if you need wisdom to help you do something God has asked you to do — just ask Him and He'll *abundantly* supply you with *His* wisdom. I know that's true because the Bible says He will *liberally* give you wisdom if you just ask Him for it. That's not just someone's opinion — that's the Bible!

God never wants us to say, "I can't," because *He* can through us! I remember when I was in grade school, my teachers were always saying to us, "Don't ever say, 'I can't'"?

They taught us that we could do anything we wanted to do in life if we would just apply ourselves. They were trying to teach us that we can do anything we *believe* we can do.

If that principle is true in the natural, how much more it is true because the power of God works in our lives! The Bible says that with God all things are possible (Luke 1:37). God works through our impossibilities and helps us achieve the impossible in our lives. He turns every impossibility into a possibility.

When God promises you something, if you'll hold on to His promise, He'll make even the impossible become possible. But if you refuse to believe God's promise, those possibilities will be *im*possibilities *to you*, because without God at work in the situation, you're left with hopelessness. That's what happened to the Israelites.

Once the ten spies refused to believe God's promise that they could take their promised land, they allowed so much fear and unbelief to rule their thinking that they became negative and hopeless. Wrong thinking and wrong talking produce despair and hopelessness.

We Christians do the same thing today. When we start thinking the wrong things, we start talking wrong, and soon we start assuming things that aren't true.

Let me give you an example. You can start thinking and talking about yourself negatively, saying, "I'm not worth much." If you keep thinking and talking like that, soon you'll start believing it.

Maybe something happened to make you critical of yourself or someone said something that hurt your feelings. Maybe you had a bad experience that made you wonder if people really like you, so you started thinking bad thoughts about yourself.

For instance, have you ever walked into a room where people were talking and when they saw you, they stopped talking? You assume that they are talking about you, so you go out and tell someone else, "Those people are talking about me!" But how do you really know that? You didn't hear what they said!

And if that situation happens more than once, you can get a complex thinking, *What in the world is going on! Everywhere I go, people are talking about me!*

You can get yourself so far down in depression that it would take three Mack trucks to pull you out! But maybe those people love you and were planning a special surprise party for you, and they didn't want you to know about it. Or maybe they stopped talking when you walked in so they could say hello to you. Or *maybe* it was just a coincidence!

The point is, we can allow ourselves to get so despondent and disappointed by circumstances that we start thinking the worst about every situation.

Wrong thinking will get you talking wrong and believing wrong. Wrong believing, wrong thinking, and wrong talking cause confusion and will wreak havoc in every area of your life.

You should know that God already has every one of your problems solved if you'll just trust Him. He promised that He would cause you to triumph in every situation (2 Cor. 2:14). So you need to stop meditating on doubt and unbelief! If you meditate on negative thoughts, you'll just work yourself into a frenzy.

That's what happened to the Israelites. They saw the walled cities and the giants in the land, and instead of focusing on God, they got their eyes on the circumstances. Actually, the Israelites got their eyes off what God said — His personal *promise* to them — and they got their eyes on the circumstances of life.

We Christians do the same thing today. If you are ever going to receive what God has for you in life, you're going to have to keep your eyes on God and get them off your problems. Get your eyes off the test or trial and keep them on the goal — God's promise to you.

It's the same way in the natural realm. You can't

focus on two separate objects at the same time. For example, if you're playing basketball and you're dribbling the ball down the court, you won't be able to make a basket if you're looking at the stands to see who's watching you shoot the ball!

If you're dribbling the basketball down the court, but you keep looking to see if your girlfriend is watching you, you leave yourself wide open for your opponent to steal the ball from you.

It's the same way in your Christian walk. If your eyes are on anything but the goal — God and His promise to you — you'll allow the devil to steal your goods!

When you're playing basketball and you've got the ball, you've got to keep your eyes on the goal, which is making a basket. You do everything you can to protect the ball, because the opponent guarding you will try to steal it from you.

You have to do that with the blessings of God too. Whatever God says belongs to you, you have to guard and protect it so the devil won't steal it from you. You keep your eyes on the goal — the promise of God — but you guard the blessings of God in your heart.

The Israelites didn't do that. They didn't guard what God had promised them, and they didn't keep their eyes on the goal. Instead, they murmured and complained, and that got their eyes off the goal.

When the ten spies told the other Israelites that it was impossible to possess the Promised Land, the children of Israel got together in a committee and began murmuring and complaining against Moses and Aaron (Num. 14:2).

The Israelites cried and complained, "Boo hoo! Poor ole us! We're out here in the middle of the desert. At least we had a roof over our heads in Egypt. When we were in the sin and bondage of Egypt, at least we had real food to eat. But we don't have anything but manna out here in this wilderness with this Jehovah God fellow."

> **NUMBERS 14:1-3**
> **1   And all the congregation lifted up their voice, and cried; and the people wept that night.**
> **2   And all the children of Israel murmured against Moses and against Aaron: and the whole congregation said unto them, WOULD GOD THAT WE HAD DIED IN THE LAND OF EGYPT! OR WOULD GOD WE HAD DIED IN THIS WILDERNESS!**
> **3   And wherefore hath the Lord brought us unto this land, to fall by the sword, that our wives and our children should be a prey? WERE IT NOT BETTER FOR US TO RETURN INTO EGYPT?**

These Israelites acted just like many Christians do today. They'd traveled all the way from the land of Egypt where they were in sin and bondage. God had supernaturally taken care of them, and they were finally on the threshold of entering into the land that God had promised them. But then they allowed an evil report to get them discouraged.

All the people lifted up their voices and wept. An evil report causes despair, and it causes people to stumble in their faith. The Israelites said, "It would have been bet-

ter for us to have died in Egypt than to have come out
here in the desert to try to follow God" (Num. 14:2).

Think about that statement! What a negative thing
for the Israelites to say, especially since God had performed so many wonders for them! They were really
saying that they would have been better off if they'd all
died in *sin*, because Egypt is a type of sin.

Do you see that once you think wrong and believe
wrong, your talk goes crazy! What's really bad is that a
negative report shows your lack of faith in God. It
shows what's really in your heart.

I've heard some believers say almost the same thing
as the Israelites. Sometimes when the devil gets believers entangled in the crises of life, they cry and complain, "Oh, God, why me? Oh, God, why did *You* let this
happen to me?"

But God didn't cause your crisis. He didn't bring
that situation into your life. The Bible says that it's the
thief that comes to steal, kill, and destroy. Jesus came
to bring life and that more abundantly (John 10:10). It
also says that we are going to face trials and tribulations in this life because the devil is the god of this
world (2 Cor. 4:4).

Just because we walk by faith is no sign that we're
exempt from trials, tribulations, and temptations in
this life. But the Bible also said that in all of them, we
are more than conquerors (Rom. 8:37).

David said it like this in Psalm 23:4: *"Yea, though I
walk through the valley of the shadow of death, I will
fear no evil."* The word "death" in that sentence doesn't

mean the cessation of life. The expression "the shadow of death" in that scripture means that in this world where Satan is god, we see the effects of spiritual death — Satan's kingdom — all around us.

And sometimes when we walk through a crisis, it feels like we're experiencing a type of death because of the pressures the enemy brings upon us. But God promised that He would prepare a table before us in the very presence of our enemies.

PSALM 23:5
5 THOU PREPAREST A TABLE BEFORE ME in the presence of mine enemies: thou anointest my head with oil; my cup runneth over.

You see, no matter what you go through in life, as long as you stay close to God, He will help you and protect you. And He'll show you how to come out of every situation as a *victor*, not a *victim*.

God has made many provisions for His children to be able to possess their promise land. And even when we walk through what seems to be a wilderness, God provides a table of abundant provision for us.

As long as you stay at the table of God's provision, even though the enemy is all around you, he can't get to you because he can't come to the table! Just sit down at the Lord's table of provision, and let the Lord take care of you.

Some believers are seated at the table all right. But they're worrying about the enemy or they're worried about the cares of this life. Quit worrying about all that! *Just stay at the table and eat the Word.*

Learn how to enjoy life because you're seated in heavenly places with the King of kings and the Lord of lords. No enemy can come to that table. Just stay at the table of the Lord's provision, and the enemy can't get an inroad into your life!

If the children of Israel had really grabbed ahold of God's provision for them, they could have walked right in and taken possession of their land. And the enemy couldn't have done a thing about it.

But, you see, so many times when we suffer a great disappointment like the Israelites did, if we're not careful to keep our thoughts and words in line with God's Word, our unrenewed mind will take over.

An unrenewed mind left unchecked will run rampant, thinking negative thoughts. That opens a door to the devil. Then we start talking negative words and make the situation even worse.

If we follow after our own thoughts and feelings, we'll always get into despair. Have you ever heard believers say, "I was better off before I ever got saved!"

That's murmuring against God Himself. That's saying God isn't big enough to do what He said He'd do. Don't ever utter those words! It grieves the Spirit of God and hinders Him from bringing to pass His best for your life.

Watch unbelief in your life, because unbelief stirs up rebellion. The Israelites got into so much unbelief that rebellion broke out in their ranks, and they were ready to break out into mutiny against Moses and Aaron.

They wanted to install a new commander and go back
to the bondage of Egypt. Can you imagine wanting to go
back to sin and bondage!

NUMBERS 14:4
**4   And they said one to another, Let us make a
captain, and let us return into Egypt.**

Too many Christians are like that today. They walk
with God as long as everything in life is going smoothly.
But let the devil throw the first temptation or trial
their way, and they're ready to go back into their life of
sin. Or if someone says the wrong thing to them, it
causes them to backslide, and they end up back on the
devil's junk heap!

You won't be able to possess what God has for you if
you're always allowing people to cause you to stumble.
But, thank God, you don't ever have to end up on the
devil's junk heap!

If people have done you wrong, let God deal with them.
Just make sure you keep yourself on the right track with
God. Make sure your *own* heart is right with God!

That's what Moses and Aaron did when the
Israelites came against them and criticized them. They
didn't worry about the other Israelites. They just fell on
their faces and humbled themselves before God. They
didn't try to prove they were right. They just gave the
situation over to God.

NUMBERS 14:5-10
5   THEN MOSES AND AARON FELL ON THEIR

FACES before all the assembly of the congregation of the children of Israel.

6 And Joshua the son of Nun, and Caleb the son of Jephunneh, which were of them that searched the land, rent their clothes:

7 And they spake unto all the company of the children of Israel, saying, The land, which we passed through to search it, is an exceeding good land.

8 If the Lord delight in us, then he will bring us into this land, and give it us; a land which floweth with milk and honey.

9 Only rebel not ye against the Lord, neither fear ye the people of the land; FOR THEY ARE BREAD FOR US: THEIR DEFENCE IS DEPARTED FROM THEM, and the Lord is with us: fear them not.

10 But all the congregation bade stone them with stones. And the glory of the Lord appeared in the tabernacle of the congregation before all the children of Israel.

Joshua spoke to the Israelites, and said, "Don't worry about those people. They're bread for us!"

Think about a slice of bread. You can go get a slice of bread anytime you want to and do whatever you want to with it. You can step on it or throw it away — it doesn't make any difference. The poor ole bread can't do anything about it because you've got the controlling authority over it.

That's what Joshua was trying to tell these people. "I don't care how big and strong those giants are, the Lord is bigger. It doesn't matter how big their cities are or how many walls they've got, don't rebel against the Lord because those people are nothing to God. With God we can do anything!"

Instead of relying on God, those Israelites must have been trusting in their bows and arrows to conquer the Promised Land. They got into doubt and unbelief because they knew *they* couldn't do it. They were relying on their own strength. Anytime we rely on our own strength, it produces despair.

Besides, that's not what God had said. If they'd just believed God's promise to them, they could have leaned back in the arms of God and walked right into every one of those fortified enemy cities — giants or no giants — and taken their promised land with ease.

Joshua and Caleb were the only two Israelites who believed God. They kept telling the people how to get the blessings of God to work for them. They said, *"If the Lord delight in us, then he will bring us into this land, and give it us; a land which floweth with milk and honey"* (Num. 14:8).

Psalm 37:4 tells us the same thing today: *"Delight thyself also in the Lord; and he shall give thee the desires of thine heart."* But the Lord doesn't delight in murmuring and complaining.

To keep their faith strong in the midst of all the Israelites' doubt and unbelief, Joshua and Caleb probably kept remembering all the wonders and miracles God had performed for them in the past. They probably thought about all of God's past victories.

For example, Joshua and Caleb could still remember back to the Israelites' flight from Egypt, and the Egyptian army following hard after them. They remembered being confronted with an impossible situation — the

Egyptians in hot pursuit closing in behind them and the Red Sea stretched out before them.

There was only one way out of that impossible situation and it was *God*! Joshua and Caleb could remember when God instructed Moses to take the rod in his hand and stretch it out across the Red Sea.

As Moses obeyed, the Red Sea parted and the Israelites walked across on dry ground. When the Egyptians tried to follow them, they were swallowed up in the wall of water that came crashing down on top of them.

Joshua and Caleb remembered their past victories in God. They renewed their minds by recalling the awesome ability of God and the mighty acts He'd already performed for them.

Because their minds were renewed to the awesome ability of God, Joshua and Caleb knew it wasn't hard for God to bring them into their Promised Land.

Some of us need to renew our minds to the awesome ability of God too! Then we wouldn't have any trouble knowing that nothing is impossible with God (Luke 1:37). Too often we look at ourselves and think there's no way God could bring us into our promised land. But we shouldn't be looking at ourselves in the first place — we should be looking at *God*!

Joshua and Caleb knew the secret of keeping their eyes focused on God. That's why they could talk faith to the people — the God-kind of faith. In effect, Joshua told the Israelites, "The enemy isn't our problem because their defense is departed from them. The land is ours to possess" (Num. 14:9).

Have you ever thought about it? The enemy isn't our problem either because he's already been defeated by Jesus Christ at Calvary! Our only problem is *us*. Are we going to obey God and do what He told us to do? Or are we just going to allow fear and doubt and unbelief to overtake us like the Israelites did?

Joshua spoke the God-kind of faith! He showed what he believed in his heart by what he *said*. When we run into a test or a trial in our own lives, we need to remember to speak faith-filled words — words filled with the God-kind of faith.

Don't be weak in faith like the Israelites. Instead of complaining about the circumstances, say to yourself, "I refuse to fear! God has already redeemed me from the hand of the enemy! Satan's defense has departed from him. If I'll just trust God, I can possess my promised land!"

Like Joshua and Caleb, remember all the wonders God has performed in your life. Remember when God saved you and delivered you out of Satan's kingdom.

Think back to the many times when the Lord answered your prayers and delivered you out of trying times and difficult circumstances. Get your mind renewed to God's goodness and great power. Remember the God who is more than enough to meet your every need!

Speak faith-filled words like Joshua and Caleb. I want you to get ahold of the God-kind of faith in action. Joshua and Caleb possessed their Promised Land by what they *said*. They were determined to follow God and take Him at His Word — that's living by faith.

Actually, the faith that Joshua and Caleb spoke sounded a lot like old Abraham's faith.

> **ROMANS 4:20,21**
> **20 He** [Abraham] **staggered not at the promise of God through unbelief; but was strong in faith, giving glory to God;**
> **21 And BEING FULLY PERSUADED THAT, WHAT HE HAD PROMISED, HE WAS ABLE ALSO TO PERFORM.**

Basically, Joshua and Caleb spoke the same faith-filled words as Abraham: "We are fully persuaded that God is well able and capable of doing what He has promised He would do."

But instead of believing what God had said, the other Israelites believed only what they could see. They were going contrary to one of the faith principles the Apostle Paul would write many, many years later in the New Testament. Paul said, "For we walk by *faith, not by sight*" (2 Cor. 5:7). The Israelites walked by sight, not by faith.

Joshua and Caleb didn't walk by sight — just by natural eyesight alone. They'd seen the same land and the same giants the other ten spies had seen. But Joshua and Caleb walked by faith, not by what things looked like in the natural.

But I want you to notice what happens when people begin to walk by faith. When Joshua and Caleb took a strong faith stand on God's Word, the Israelites cried out against them, saying, "Let's stone these rebels" (Num. 14:10).

It took a supernatural, divine intervention from God to keep Joshua and Caleb from getting stoned by the Israelites that day. The glory of the Lord shone in the tabernacle before all the children of Israel. It was only the glory of God that saved the lives of Joshua and Caleb.

How many times have we needed God's glory to intervene and shine on our lives to deliver us from difficult situations!

How many of you have felt like people wanted to stone you because you took a stand on God's Word? Of course, people didn't literally stone you. But maybe some people forsook you and separated themselves from you because you chose to believe God. Maybe some of you were even turned out of churches when you began to take God at His Word.

And sometimes believers receive a lot of verbal stones. Sometimes I think verbal stones do a lot more damage than a real stone can do. If someone literally threw a stone at you, that bruise would eventually heal, and after a while, it would be gone.

But many times you have to continue to stand in faith to overcome some of the verbal bruises you've endured. You have to stand on the Word of God to keep those words from coming back to influence your life, because they registered on your heart and mind.

But I want you to notice something else in this passage of Scripture. When God is behind what you are saying and doing, He demonstrates Himself in a mighty way on your behalf like He did with Joshua and Caleb.

If what you're doing is of God, people can't stop it unless *you* just give up. The Bible said that the gates of hell can't prevail against the Church (Matt. 16:18). So just rest in God's promise to you, knowing that God will protect you against any verbal stones the devil might try to throw your way.

When the Israelites rose up against Joshua and Caleb to stone them, that's when the Lord really got upset. The Israelites provoked the Lord to anger that day.

The Lord said to Moses, ". . . *How long will this people provoke me? and how long will it be ere they believe me, for all the signs which I have shewed among them?*" (Num. 14:11).

You see, God has emotions. Where do you think we get our emotions from? The Bible tells us that we were formed in the image and likeness of God. God breathed the breath of life into us. We have emotions, and God has emotions, too, because we are made in His image.

Jesus said, "If you've seen Me, you've seen the Father" (John 14:9). Jesus had emotions too. Jesus wept, He laughed, and He got angry. In the temple when the money-changers were making His Father's house a house of merchandise, Jesus Christ the Son of God got angry (John 2:16)!

So the Lord said to Moses about the Israelites, "Moses, how long do you think I'm going to put up with this bunch of unbelieving rascals? How long will it be before they start believing Me?"

It's possible to provoke God. Doubt and unbelief provoke God. Believers provoke God when they refuse to live by faith in God's Word or when they refuse to walk with Him. God is just waiting for Christians to believe Him and take Him at His Word so He can move mightily in their lives.

You can understand why the Israelites' continual doubt and unbelief would provoke the Lord. Look what the Lord had done for them. How many times did He supernaturally provide for them in their long journey from Egypt to the Promised land. He delivered them from their enemies again and again.

Many times God showed His wonders and miracles to the Israelites, and He demonstrated His great power to them. He led them supernaturally by a pillar of cloud by day and a pillar of fire by night.

When Moses was on Mt. Sinai, God gave the Israelites the Law, which He wrote with His own finger. God visited the mountain with fire and smoke and showed them His awesome power.

Moses and Aaron had intervened for the Israelites time and time again because their disobedience provoked God's wrath. Otherwise, God would have destroyed them at Mt. Sinai when they made the golden calf to worship (Exod. 32:1-35). And here the Israelites were tempting God again by murmuring and complaining against Him.

Just like the Israelites, we need to be careful about what we *say*. Sometimes when believers don't see the move and the power of God manifested immediately when they pray, they begin to complain, "Well, I guess God isn't going to do anything for us anymore."

Be careful what you say! Good or bad, you will eventually receive what you believe in your heart and say with your mouth!

When we get into doubt and unbelief, I wonder if the Lord feels about us like He did about the Israelites: "How much do I have to do for them before they will believe Me and take Me at My Word?"

There are consequences for rebellion, disobedience, and murmuring and complaining. God finally had to pronounce His judgment on the Israelites. He said, ". . . *I will smite them with the pestilence, and disinherit them, and will make of thee a greater nation and mightier than they*" (Num. 14:12).

People say, "God would never disinherit the Israelites because He's such a loving God." Yes, He is a loving God, but He's also a righteous God. And He'd had enough of the Israelites' constant unbelief, murmuring, and complaining. When you love someone, you discipline him. Parents who don't discipline their children don't love them.

But Moses began to intercede on the Israelites' behalf, and God in His great mercy pardoned them (Num. 14:13-20). Moses had to pray on behalf of those Israelites just like many pastors today who have to pray for some of their murmuring church members.

For example, sometimes church members rise up and begin murmuring and complaining about their pastor. If you are murmuring against your pastor or the leaders of your church, don't expect God to do anything for you. And don't expect faith to work for you, because your criticism will nullify your faith. The Bible says faith works by love (Gal. 5:6).

If believers would pray for their leaders instead of criticizing them, God would work things out. Sometimes believers murmur and complain about their pastor because they're in doubt and unbelief or because they believe someone else's negative report. That's exactly what happened to the children of Israel.

After all the wonders and miracles God had performed, the Israelites should have known that God was faithful to keep His Word and do what He had promised. After all, He had faithfully delivered them out of every situation in the past.

But if you study the flight of the children of Israel out of Egypt to the Promised Land, you find out that ten times the Israelites provoked God with their doubt and unbelief.

> **NUMBERS 14:22,23**
> **22 Because all those men which have seen my glory, and my miracles, which I did in Egypt and in the wilderness, and HAVE TEMPTED ME NOW THESE TEN TIMES, and have not hearkened to my voice;**
> **23 Surely they shall not see the land which I sware unto their fathers, neither shall any of them that provoked me see it.**

The Israelites suffered a divine penalty because they didn't believe God in their hearts, and they refused to speak in line with His promise. When Moses interceded on their behalf, God said, "All right, I'll spare them. But they shall never see the land that I promised them."

NUMBERS 14:26-32
26 And the Lord spake unto Moses and unto Aaron, saying,
27 How long shall I bear with this EVIL CONGRE-GATION, which murmur against me? I have heard the murmurings of the children of Israel, which they murmur against me.
28 Say unto them, AS TRULY AS I LIVE, SAITH THE LORD, AS YE HAVE SPOKEN IN MINE EARS, SO WILL I DO TO YOU:
29 Your carcases shall fall in this wilderness; and all that were numbered of you, according to your whole number, from twenty years old and upward, which have murmured against me,
30 Doubtless ye shall not come into the land, concerning which I sware to make you dwell therein, save Caleb the son of Jephunneh, and Joshua the son of Nun.
31 But your little ones, which ye said should be a prey, them will I bring in, and they shall know the land which ye have despised.
32 But as for you, your carcases, they shall fall in this wilderness.

God was really saying, "This bunch of unbelieving, evil-thinking people don't believe I can do what I say I can do! But without My hand of blessing on them, they will die in the wilderness."

You see, when you get over into unbelief, you get out from under God's protective hand of blessing. Without faith in God, you don't have a defense against the devil, and the enemy has a straight shot at you.

Without faith in God, you don't have any shield of faith to hold up. Without faith, you hinder the supernatural power of God from operating in your life like

God has designed it to. Without faith in God, you are stripped of your defenses, and you are vulnerable to every attack the enemy brings along.

It takes faith to please God. It's not pleasing to God when we don't take Him at His Word. That's why God said, "If they're going to keep talking like that, I'll find people who believe Me. And I'll make them a greater and a more mighty nation than these Israelites!"

We can see exactly what God thinks about people speaking contrary to His Word and His promises. He called them an evil congregation because they talked doubt and unbelief.

God pronounced judgment against the Israelites: ". . . as ye have spoken in mine ears, so will I do to you" (v. 28).

Then He said, "All those who were twenty years and older who murmured against me will die in the wilderness." So the Israelites wandered in the wilderness forty years just because they could never get into agreement with God.

Out of that whole bunch, Caleb and Joshua were the only two who agreed with God. They were also the only ones twenty years and older who didn't die in the wilderness.

But look at the mercy of God. God said, "But your little ones, which ye said should be a prey, them will I bring in, and they shall know the land which ye have despised" (v. 31).

All those who are under twenty years old didn't

have any vote or any control of what was going on, so God didn't penalize them. The younger ones were just subject to their elders, so God didn't judge them for it. As a just God, he couldn't penalize the little ones for the doubt and unbelief of their elders.

That puts a lot of responsibility on us as parents, doesn't it? And it puts a lot of responsibility on us as elders in the church, and upon the leaders in the Body of Christ to be an example to speak what is right.

God in His mercy didn't disown the Israelites. That bunch didn't go in to the Promised Land, but they did repent later, and I believe they will be counted among those we'll see in Heaven. But they didn't get the best that God had for them down here in this life. They fell short of their Promised Land.

They made a big mistake by not following God and just accepting God's promise. Finally, God said, "You said it, so now you're going to live out the consequences of your words. What you say is what you get! Which one of us would want to live out the consequences of *our* words?

Think about it! Those who stayed in faith crossed over to inherit the Promised Land. The doubters reaped the consequences of their words and died in the wilderness. They dug their own grave with their words.

Their tombstone should have read: "Here lies those children of God who refused to believe! Here lies those who doubted God!" And over the archway of the cemetery a sign should have read, "The Graves of Those Who Doubted God."

Yes, the Israelites were still God's children. But they did not receive God's best — their Promised Land — when they were down here on this earth.

There are a lot of people today who belong to God, and they will make it to Heaven, but they're not getting the best that God has for them on this earth.

People ask, "Well, what are we going to do with those believers who can't ever seem to get ahold of what God has for them?" Remember, the Word of God says, "The *poor* you shall always have with you" (Mark 14:7).

I know this scripture refers to those who are financially poor, but I think there is another application for this verse too. The spiritually poor we will always have with us. There will always be Christians who aren't where they should be spiritually.

We can help the poor in spirit. We can help comfort them in their days down here in this life. And when they get to Heaven, they'll be able to enjoy days without sorrow. But *we* can enjoy our days on this earth right now because we know how to believe God.

When God's people do not live according to His statutes, God has to bring judgment (1 Cor. 11:29). If God's people obey Him, God grants mercy. Therefore, whether or not we ever inherit what God's promised us depends on what we *say*, what we *do*, and how we *live*.

God had to bring judgment on the Israelites because they refused to accept His Word and do what He'd told them to do.

You can see how important your words are to God!

How important it is to agree with God's Word! You may have to stand strong in faith despite everyone around you who is talking doubt and unbelief. You may have to resist the temptation to think thoughts that are filled with doubt, unbelief, and fear.

You may be the only one standing fast in faith, declaring, "I believe God!" But that's how you possess what God has promised you. You may have to speak your faith like Caleb and Joshua did even in the midst of great opposition.

But don't let the circumstances cloud your vision of what God has promised you! Don't let fear and unbelief keep you from all that your heart desires.

You don't have to bring God's promises to pass in your life. All God wants *you* to do is stay in faith and obedience.

As you get in agreement with God in every area of your life, God is more than able to bring His will to pass in your life. Go in and possess your promised land. Walk in the abundance of everything God has prepared for you!

Chapter 3
'Give Me This Mountain!'

When the twelve Israelite spies went to spy out the Promised Land, only two of them were successful. Even though all twelve saw the same things — the same inhabitants, the same giants, and the same rich abundance of the land, — Joshua and Caleb were the only ones who inherited their Promised Land.

The Success of Caleb

Let's look at one of these Israelite spies, this man Caleb, to find out the secret of his success. Caleb went on to receive his promised land. Why was he able to possess the land he'd seen forty years before?

JOSHUA 14:6-14
6   Then the children of Judah came unto Joshua in Gilgal: and Caleb the son of Jephunneh the Kenezite said unto him [Joshua], Thou knowest the thing that the Lord said unto Moses the man of God concerning me and thee in Kadesh-barnea.
7   Forty years old was I when Moses the servant of the Lord sent me from Kadesh-barnea to espy out the land; and I brought him word again as it was in mine heart.
8   Nevertheless my brethren that went up with me made the heart of the people melt: BUT I WHOLLY FOLLOWED THE LORD MY GOD.
9   And Moses sware on that day, saying, Surely the land whereon thy feet have trodden shall be

thine inheritance, and thy children's for ever,
BECAUSE THOU HAST WHOLLY FOLLOWED
THE LORD MY GOD.
10 And now, behold, the Lord hath kept me alive,
as he said, these forty and five years, even since
the Lord spake this word unto Moses, while the
children of Israel wandered in the wilderness: and
now, lo, I am this day fourscore and five years old.
11 As yet I am as strong this day as I was in the
day that Moses sent me: as my strength was then,
even so is my strength now, for war, both to go out,
and to come in.
12 NOW THEREFORE GIVE ME THIS MOUN-
TAIN, whereof the Lord spake in that day; for thou
heardest in that day how the Anakims were there,
and that the cities were great and fenced: if so be
the Lord will be with me, then I shall be able to
drive them out, as the Lord said.
13 And Joshua blessed him, and gave unto Caleb
the son of Jephunneh Hebron for an inheritance.
14 Hebron therefore became the inheritance of
Caleb the son of Jephunneh the Kenezite unto this
day, BECAUSE THAT HE WHOLLY FOLLOWED
THE LORD GOD OF ISRAEL.

Caleb Wholly Followed the Lord

This passage in Joshua 14 gives us a key to Caleb's
success. Three times the phrase is mentioned, "Caleb
wholly followed the Lord God." It was Caleb's *ability to
totally follow God* that enabled him to enter into his
promised land.

Following God completely must be important. Look
at how many other times the Bible mentions it.

DEUTERONOMY 1:36
**36 ... Caleb the son of Jephunneh; he shall see it,
and to him will I give the land that he hath trodden upon, and to his children, BECAUSE HE
HATH WHOLLY FOLLOWED THE LORD.**

NUMBERS 32:11,12
**11 Surely none of the men that came up out of
Egypt, from twenty years old and upward, shall
see the land which I sware unto Abraham, unto
Isaac, and unto Jacob; BECAUSE THEY HAVE
NOT WHOLLY FOLLOWED ME:
12 Save CALEB the son of Jephunneh the
Kenezite, and Joshua the son of Nun: for THEY
HAVE WHOLLY FOLLOWED THE LORD.**

Caleb was a success in God because he totally dedicated himself to following God. What does it mean to
wholly follow God? It means Caleb did everything God
told him to do. He *believed* what God said, he *said* what
God said, and he *did* what God said. He was in agreement with God in every area of his life.

To wholly follow the Lord means Caleb didn't follow
God halfheartedly. He didn't follow God afar off. No, he
totally followed God at every stop and every turn, completely committed to do whatever God said to do.

Caleb followed God with every ounce of his being.
And if God said to stop, he stopped. If God said to go, he
started up again. He didn't question God; he just
obeyed His instructions. This was the great key to
Caleb's success.

Also, Caleb was dedicated to a cause. What cause
was it? Was it his own cause or his own ambitions? No!

He was dedicated to the Lord's cause — to take possession of the Promised Land. He never wavered from his God-given cause and purpose.

When you know God's cause, you can get in line with God's plan. When you walk in obedience to God's plan — then you can succeed. Caleb's total obedience made it possible for him to possess his mountain, the region of Hebron.

Caleb possessed his mountain, and we're under a better covenant established upon better promises (Heb. 8:6). How much more should we be able to possess our mountain in God — the prized possession of our inheritance in Christ!

Have you ever thought about it? Most believers know more of the Word than they'll ever be able to use. And they should be free and on the mountaintop of their possession because the Word sets people free (John 8:32).

But many of them are still in bondage because they haven't wholly followed God — spirit, soul, and body.

You can't follow God afar off, halfheartedly listening for His instructions and expect to conquer your promised land. That's not the way it works. You'll have to walk closely to God, listening intently for His voice and His instructions.

Caleb Spoke the God-Kind of Faith

When the Israelites first came to the Promised Land, Caleb was one of the twelve spies sent in to spy out the Promised Land. In other words, he was called upon to undertake a dangerous assignment. One of the secrets of Caleb's success was that he not only faithfully performed his mission, but *he distinguished himself with God by his strong faith in God.*

> **NUMBERS 14:24**
> **24 But my servant Caleb, BECAUSE HE HAD ANOTHER SPIRIT WITH HIM, and hath followed me fully, him will I bring into the land whereinto he went; and his seed shall possess it.**

The Bible says Caleb "had another spirit with him." What was it? It was the spirit of faith! Caleb was a man of courage who realized that the key to success is wrapped up in the words he *said.*

Many years later, the Apostle Paul would write about the spirit of faith.

> **2 CORINTHIANS 4:13**
> **13 We having the same SPIRIT OF FAITH, according as it is written, I BELIEVED, and therefore have I SPOKEN; we also BELIEVE, and therefore SPEAK.**

The spirit of faith is the God-kind of faith that believes and speaks out its faith in God in the midst of every impossible circumstance. Caleb knew how to believe God in his heart and speak faith with his mouth. He believed the impossible could happen in God.

He never wavered from his confession, "Let's go in to possess the land because God said we can do it — not because of *who* we are or *what* we are. But we can possess what's ours because of *who God is!*"

Caleb distinguished himself by his faith in God. God could depend on him to keep his thoughts and words in agreement with God. Can God depend on *you* to get your thoughts and words in agreement with His Word?

Caleb also distinguished himself by his faith because he *stayed* in faith. Faith doesn't waver and it doesn't give up. Come what may, it's persistent. Caleb had that kind of persistent faith. He told the Israelites, "We can do anything God tells us to do! We *can* possess what rightfully belongs to us!"

And even in all those forty-five years of wandering in the wilderness with those rebellious, doubt-filled Israelites, Caleb kept his faith strong. He never relaxed his grip of faith on the land of his possession.

The God-kind of faith keeps on believing God in the face of *all* opposition. Doubt and unbelief say, "No, we can't do it. We're not able." Actually, the "I can't" of doubt and unbelief is really saying, "God isn't big enough!"

Doubt and unbelief will shut down your faith every single time. But the God-kind of faith just keeps on believing, "With God nothing is impossible!"

Actually, Caleb had the God-kind of faith that Jesus talked about in Mark 11:23,24: "*. . . whosoever shall SAY unto this mountain . . . and shall NOT DOUBT in his heart, but shall BELIEVE that those things which he SAITH shall come to pass; he shall have whatsoever he SAITH.*"

Caleb put the principles of the God-kind of faith in

Mark 11:23,24 into action long before they were written in the New Testament. And his strong, determined faith was one of the keys to his success.

Caleb knew the key of confessing the promises of God instead of the circumstances. He possessed his Promised Land because he continually put the God-kind of faith into action — his *words* agreed with God's promise to him.

If what you say with your mouth is the result of what you believe in your heart, *and it is based on God's Word*, then faith will work for you. It will work for you because that is the God-kind of faith in operation.

Believing and confessing God's Word is God's inevitable law of faith. That's the kind of faith you'll need to possess your promised land — everything that God's promised you in this life.

It's very important that what we believe in our heart and say with our mouth lines up with what *God* says. Actually, what we believe in our heart and say with our mouth is what we're going to get in this life. I'm talking about believing and talking in line with God's Word.

Caleb Never Compromised

Another reason for Caleb's success is found in the fact that *he refused to compromise what God had told him to do.* He received his inheritance because he never compromised his integrity before God or man.

Think about it! Through more than forty years of

waiting for his success walking around and around that
wilderness with those unbelieving Israelites, Caleb
could have murmured against God. He could have said,
"I don't know why I have to pay for the mistakes of
those rebellious Israelites! I didn't do anything wrong!"

But, no, Caleb never murmured against God or anyone else for that matter. He just kept believing and saying, "God said it, I believe it, and I'm going to possess
my inheritance!"

Caleb set about to accomplish what God had said
even though he was deterred and detained for many
years. It's too bad some believers today don't have that
kind of tenacious faith!

For example, some believers today feel that they're
too old to receive what God promised them. Maybe
they've been detained by the circumstances of life, so
they think there's no hope for them to inherit God's
promises.

But look at Caleb! He was 85 years old when he
finally possessed his promised land. He never gave up.
And because he never gave up, never compromised, and
never complained against God — he received everything God had for him. If he had compromised his faith
and his integrity, he never would have received the
promise of God for his life.

This should be a lesson to us! We'd better beware of
compromise, complaining, and murmuring. Those
things will cause us to forfeit our promised land and the
promises of God that rightfully belong to us.

Don't compromise! Friends, we're going to have to

learn to keep our body under authority to our spirit if we want God's best on this earth. We can't compromise and expect to receive God's best. A lot of believers say, "Well, my spirit is right with God. It's my body that's sinning."

But according to the Bible, the spirit of man on the inside is supposed to take control and bring man's body under subjection and into line with the Word of God.

Many believers believe in prosperity, faith, and healing. And thank God for our redemption in all those areas. Those blessings belong to us because they're in the Word.

But it's time we realized that sin is sin. And sin will keep you out of your promised land, which is God's best for you in every area of your life.

Yes, we've got to be positive and think and teach what's positive. I'm not trying to get on the negative side of things.

But people who call themselves children of God should humble themselves and begin to live right before God and quit doing some of the things the world does. We can't compromise; we've got to shun the very appearance of evil.

Sometimes I think some Charismatic Christians try to come as close as they can to wrongdoing and get by with it. Then they wonder why they can't possess the promises of God. We are to be separate from the world. We have to live in the world, but we do not have to think and act like the world.

You ask, "What does that have to do with success and receiving my promised land in this life?" It has everything to do with success in God. You can't compromise and receive God's best in this life. It just won't work. I'm not talking about how long or short your hair is or whether you wear long or short sleeves.

Yes, Christians should dress in a dignified way, not sensually or sleazy. The Bible talks about our outward adorning, and it says that we're to dress modestly (1 Peter 3:4).

But, actually, that's not the main point Peter was trying to get across in that verse. The Bible is telling us not to spend all our time taking care of the outward man, and pay no attention to adorning the inward man.

And too many people preach confession, confession, confession like that's the only way you receive from God. But, friends, making all the right faith confessions won't do any good if you're not wholly following God. Faith confessions won't profit you if you compromise yourself and compromise your integrity before God and man.

A lot of Christians run around hollering, "Bless God! I believe God for my petition. I confess that I receive what I desire." But they might as well be whistling "Dixie"! That's about all the good they're going to get out of their confessions because they've compromised themselves by harboring sin in their lives.

Now, of course, if you've made a mistake, you need to ask God to forgive you according to First John 1:9. Then get in line with God, and go on and forget the past. Once you've really repented, the past is gone, it's over, and it's done with.

But if you don't really repent of wrongdoing, it will keep you out of your promised land. By the same token, if you don't let go of the past once you've repented, it will also hinder you from receiving God's best in this life because it will hold you back from progressing in God.

Friends, it's time we realize that the day of compromise is over. We need to stand uprightly and walk uprightly before God. Your victory will come when you wholly follow God.

Caleb wholly followed God and he refused to compromise. He was totally committed to God's plan. When the Israelites turned against him and wanted to stone him for his faith in God, Caleb didn't compromise what he believed, and he didn't change what he was saying. Those are the qualities that made him a success.

Caleb Submitted to Godly Leadership

I want you to notice something else that made Caleb a success. Once Joshua succeeded Moses, Caleb became a staunch follower of Joshua. There was no rivalry between them, even though both of them had been spies in Canaan.

Caleb's submission to Joshua's leadership was another reason for his success in God and his ability to possess what God had promised him.

Caleb could have complained, "Why wasn't I chosen to be the leader? Why did God choose Joshua? I believed God too! I came back with a good report too! So why didn't God pick me to be the leader!"

In fact, Numbers 13 and 14 actually records more of what Caleb said about Canaan than what Joshua said about it. And Caleb is the one who got the children of Israel quieted down so he could talk to them — yet Joshua was the one God chose to succeed Moses.

Studying the meager details of Caleb's life, we find that he was one of the strong fighting men. And he backed Joshua's every move during the years that followed the Israelites' journey into the Promised Land.

Caleb's attitude was, "All right, Lord, you chose Joshua. I will wholly follow You. That means I will be submissive to Joshua as the leader *You* have chosen. I'll help him fulfill the vision you have for him."

Many people don't realize this, but part of wholly following God is being submissive to the leaders *God* has chosen.

Yes, you may have more qualifications than they do. You may be a better speaker than they are and a better prayer warrior. You may even be better looking than they are!

In fact, you may be better than they are in every respect. But for whatever reason, God has chosen them, and if you are to wholly follow God, you must come into submission to *God's* choice.

That's true spiritual authority. You'll never be able to possess your promised land unless you can submit yourself to spiritual leadership. God taps people on the shoulder, so to speak, and calls them to do specific jobs for Him. And I've noticed that the way God thinks and chooses is a lot different from the way I would choose!

But, you see, God has supernatural abilities we don't have. We can only see the outward appearance, but the Bible says that the Lord looks on the heart (1 Sam. 16:7). Often, people's hearts are different from what they show on the outside, and God can see their heart *attitudes*.

Also, people may be passed over by God because they aren't receptive to the Lord when He taps them on the shoulder to do something for Him. Many times they're too busy doing their own thing to hear His Voice.

For example, they may be running their own ministry or missionary program, and they are too busy or too caught up with natural things to hear the Lord when He speaks. So the Lord has no alternative but to go to someone else who is praying, "Lord, I'll do anything You want me to do."

We can be working so hard for God and giving out so much all the time that we actually miss the Spirit of God when He wants us to make a change! Sometimes we get too busy to hear Him when He says, "Make a change. Don't go straight; turn right instead."

Because we're not as sensitive to His voice as we should be, sometimes we keep on plowing straight ahead. And before you know it, we're butting our heads against a wall and we can't figure out why.

The reason we've come to a dead end is that God turned right, but we kept on going straight! That's why

Paul warns us not to become weary in well-doing. We'll never be able to receive all that God has for us in this life if we spend all our time in the natural realm.

We've probably all made the mistake at one time or another of being so caught up in well-doing that we failed to spend enough time with God. When we don't spend time with God, it's harder to be in tune to hear His voice. If we follow Him afar off, His voice can become hard for us to distinguish. How can we wholly follow God if we can't even hear His voice?

I just thank God for His mercy and grace, which allow us to repent and ask forgiveness. I'm willing to say, "I missed it," and then turn around and retrace my steps to where I made the mistake in the first place and start over from there. That's part of wholly following the Lord.

When we make a mistake, we should have Caleb's attitude. Think about it. One key that enabled Caleb to possess his promised land was his godly attitude.

He didn't go around stirring up trouble, saying, "Look, God, I'm not going to submit to someone who's just a spy like I was! You should have chosen me as Moses' successor. After all, I'm one of the original twelve spies, and I taught the people more than anyone else. I'm important, so I believe I ought to be the leader."

In this day and age, I've seen many leaders who for different reasons have not been able to flow with the move of God when God went in a little different direction. Yet some of them got mad and jealous when someone else started to do something for God.

For example, maybe another preacher comes to their town, starts a church, and in two years the new church has 400 people. That makes the first pastor jealous because he's been there for 30 years and is running 60 people in a town of 10,000. I've seen that happen!

Then when someone else really wants to do something for God, he complains, "Well, I don't know why these people came to *my* town, trying to take over *my* territory!"

Yes, there's such a thing as ministerial ethics, and that means you don't go down the street or right next door and start another church. Normally, it wouldn't be right to go into a community that's not large enough to support two works.

Besides, faith doesn't stir up strife. Faith just wholly follows God, expecting God to lead wherever He chooses. Caleb had that kind of spirit of faith and dedication to God. He said, "Not my will, Lord. Whatever *You* say. You say it, Lord, and I'll do it." Caleb never argued with the Lord about what God wanted him to do.

Sometimes when God asks some of us to do something for Him, we reply, "Lord, are You sure You *really* want me to do that? Now, Lord, I believe it would be better if we did this instead."

But when the Lord gives you the plan and instructs you how to possess your promised land, don't go back to Him and say, "Now, Lord, I don't really see it that way. I think we ought to do it *my* way."

If God wanted to do it *your* way, He would have told you! If He specifically tells you to do something a certain way, then do it that way! He's telling you to do it that way because He knows it will work. Wholly following God is carrying out God's plan in God's way, regardless of *your* opinion.

Caleb Possessed His Mountain!

After the children of Israel had been in the Promised Land a while, Caleb was finally able to claim the land Moses had promised to him years before.

> **JOSHUA 14:10-13**
> **10 And now, behold, the Lord hath kept me alive, as he said, these forty and five years, even since the Lord spake this word unto Moses, while the children of Israel wandered in the wilderness: and now, lo, I am this day fourscore and five years old.**
> **11 As yet I am as strong this day as I was in the day that Moses sent me: as my strength was then, even so is my strength now, for war, both to go out, and to come in.**
> **12 NOW THEREFORE GIVE ME THIS MOUNTAIN, whereof the Lord spake in that day; for thou heardest in that day how the Anakims were there, and that the cities were great and fenced: if so be the Lord will be with me, then I shall be able to drive them out, as the Lord said.**
> **13 And Joshua blessed him, and gave unto Caleb the son of Jephunneh Hebron for an inheritance.**

I can just see 85-year-old Caleb as he walked up to Joshua, the commander-in-chief, saying something like this: "Joshua, I've been with you from the time we went in to spy out the land. I've fought beside you, and I've honored your commands.

"Now you are dividing the land, and I'm asking you to give me the land the Lord promised me when we first spied out the land. Joshua, I want the mountain that God promised to give me 40 years ago."

The Bible doesn't say so, but maybe Joshua reminded Caleb, "But, Caleb, the fortress of the giants is still in that mountain. Besides, you were 40 years old when Moses promised you that mountain!"

But I can just see the 85-year-old faith man, Caleb, standing tall and declaring, "I may be forty-five years older than I was when we first came here to spy out the land, but I'm just as good a man as I was then, because God has sustained me.

"My God is the One I'm depending on! And because God is my strength, my strength has not abated, nor has my eyesight dimmed. My trust and my ability are in God!"

Caleb said in effect, "Besides, God is the One who is going to deliver those ungodly giants into my hands, not me! I'm not going to do anything in my own strength. It's not by *my* might, nor by *my* power, but it's by the Spirit of God. Give me this mountain!"

I can just imagine Joshua's reply to Caleb: "That's all I wanted to hear! Go on over and possess your mountain." So Caleb claimed Hebron for his inheritance.

Notice that Caleb didn't ask for an easy place. A

mountain isn't an easy place to try to produce crops or raise herds. Caleb didn't ask for the land around Jericho, nor did he ask for the area around Ai, both of which had already been subdued by the Israelites. Caleb wanted his mountain!

It seems like people today want something fast and easy — zip open the package, put it in the microwave oven for five minutes, and you've got a whole meal. It seems there's no such thing anymore as spending time in the kitchen fixing a good meal from scratch.

And that worldly, lazy attitude has even crept into the Church! Too many believers today say, "Lord, give me this mountain," but they want it served to them on a silver platter. They don't want to lift a finger or engage in any stand of faith to get it!

But if Caleb had not had "another spirit" — a spirit of faith — he wouldn't have asked for that mountain. He probably would have asked for something easy like the peaceful plains of Jericho. He could have built a city on the plains with no trouble. Knowing he would face some resistance to possessing his mountain, Caleb still asked, "Give me this mountain!"

Some believers like to say, "Oh, we don't need to fight any battles. Everything we want will just come to us in life."

But I want to warn you that if you aren't having to stand in faith against the attacks of the enemy, you'd better check up on your spiritual condition! If the devil is leaving you alone, it's because you're not living in line with God's Word (2 Tim. 3:12).

Remember this: *If there are no battles, there are no victories!*

Throughout the Epistles, the Apostle Paul cautioned us about trials and tribulation, tests and battles. But Paul said, "I thank my God because in Christ I am always a victor in them all!"

What mountains do *you* want today?

Don't answer, "Oh, Brother, I just want to sit down and rest awhile."

You're not going to receive anything from God with a lazy attitude like that. You can have any mountain you decide you want to take *if God has promised it to you.* But don't try to take what isn't promised to you in God's Word. That's where a lot of people today are getting into trouble with their faith.

A lot of people are hollering, "You *faith* people who believe the Word so strongly are just trying to manipulate God to make Him do things for you."

No! That wouldn't be faith! People who say that haven't listened to what we really teach. We don't manipulate God! God can't be manipulated by humanity. God cannot be manipulated by anything, for He is *God.*

But I'm going to tell you a truth. If God said it, I can believe it, and I can *have it* because it belongs to me.

There is a great difference between trying to manipulate God, and reaching out to take ahold of something He's already said belongs to you. God said that those of us who are born again possess an inheritance in Christ. Can we take God at His Word or not? Of course we can!

God goes to great lengths in the Word of God to tell us that we are His spiritual children and that we can have whatever He's promised us. The Bible says that as many as are led by the Spirit of God, they are the sons of God (Rom. 8:14). And the Bible says that as sons of God, we have the right and the privilege to claim what is ours in Christ (2 Cor. 1:20).

Even under the Old Covenant, Caleb knew he had the right and the privilege to claim his inheritance in God because God had already promised him that mountain. *Faith is just tapping into what already belongs to you.*

What mountain do you want to possess that God has promised you? You can have it, whether it is healing, prosperity, the baptism in the Holy Spirit, or any of the benefits of your redemption in Christ.

Just remember this. In the Old Testament, there were literal giants that opposed the children of Israel and tried to prevent them from possessing their Promised Land. Under the New Covenant, there aren't any *physical* giants that oppose us, but there are *spiritual* giants that want to oppose everything God desires to do for us.

So you will have to stand in faith against those spiritual giants — Satan and his hosts (Eph. 6:12). But always remember that they are defeated foes! Jesus already conquered them for you. Now all you have to do is stand against them with faith in God's Word.

And after you've faith-fought your way up the mountain of your promised possession by using God's

Word, then you can roll the heads of those giants back down the hill, because Satan is defeated! You only need to stand on your covenant rights against him.

Once you're standing on top of your mountain, plant your feet firmly on what belongs to you in God! Erect the flag of your inheritance in Christ. Then you will be able to take a deep breath of those mountain breezes — far away from the smog and pollution that's down in the valley of despair.

You see, by choosing that mountain, old Caleb was really saying, "I'm not going to live down in the valley with all its problems. I'm going to live up on the mountaintop of victory. And in my heart I'm going to stay as close to God as I can. I'm going to stay up on the mountaintop with God."

That's what Lot should have done. Remember Lot chose the plains of Jordan because they were well watered and beautiful (Gen. 13:10,11). But they were close to the cities of Sodom and Gomorrah, and look at all the trouble that caused him!

Lot wanted the easy way out. When Abraham and Lot were dividing up the land in their day, Lot said, "I want to take the plains. Man, look at that grass! I won't have to worry about my herds getting lost in the ravines. I won't have to worry about all the bad weather in the mountains. I'll have good weather down here on the plains all the time."

So Lot took the plains, and Abraham was left with the hill country. But when all was said and done, Lot lost everything but his own life and the lives of his two daughters. He only had time to flee from Sodom with his life. He lost his wife, his servants, his home, his inheritance, and everything else. And he had to start all over again.

Don't be like Lot! Don't always choose the easy way! In other words, don't just take the path of least resistance. Talk to God and find out what mountain *He* has for you to possess.

Then begin to proclaim, "God has given me this mountain! He's given me my inheritance in Christ! I can do all things through Christ who strengthens me!"

Of course, when you begin to proclaim, "Give me this mountain!" someone is probably going to reply, "Hey, don't you know there are giants over there!" And the devil will see to it that someone comes to discourage you with an evil report of doubt and unbelief to try to get you to change your mind!

That's when you must know who you are in Christ, and you must wholly follow the Lord. That's when you must know that the Word of *God* is your source of power, not the words *people* say.

People, even well-meaning believers, may tell you, "I know someone else who tried to take that mountain, and look at him now! He's defeated."

You'll have to stand strong in your faith in God and declare, "I can't be influenced by someone else's failure. Give me this mountain! I'm determined to possess what belongs to me in Christ."

People will question you, asking, "Why do you want *this* mountain?"

Just tell them, "Because *God* said I could have it for my inheritance — that's why I want it!"

That's exactly what Caleb did. He stood against all opposition, even the years of wandering in the wilderness with a bunch of unbelieving Israelites, so he could possess what rightfully belonged to him.

Caleb understood the God-kind of faith. He wasn't weak in faith; he was strong in faith. Mountain-taking is not for the weak in faith. It's for the strong-hearted. It's for those who are strong in faith, strong in the Spirit of God, and strong in their commitment to God.

Mountain-taking is not for those who are afraid to skin their knees from trying to climb up the mountainside of their possession either. As you climb your mountain, you may stumble a few times and have to get back up and get going again. But if you're a mountain-taker, you'll have the perseverance to do it!

Mountain-taking is not for those who want to take the easy way out. It's not for those who want to stop every five minutes and rest. Taking the mountain of possession that God has for you sometimes takes strenuous effort!

But when you finally reach the top of that mountain, what a thrill of victory you'll experience! That feeling of accomplishment is hard to put into words.

It's like when you look into the face of your newborn child for the first time, and you know that your baby is part of your flesh and blood.

Something happens inside of you that's hard to put

into words because there are no words to express that kind of joy.

God wants you to experience the sense of joy and accomplishment that comes with taking your mountain — possessing what rightfully belongs to you in Christ. Don't settle for second best. Second best says, "I don't deserve anything but second best because I'm not good enough for the best that God has for me."

You *are* good enough because of who you are in Christ! Besides, you're not going to take that mountain in your own strength anyway.

It's not by *your* might, nor by *your* power alone that you'll take that mountain. It's by the might and the power of the Spirit of God working with you and through you. Together, you and the Holy Spirit become an explosive force for God.

When the natural and the supernatural come together, they become an explosive force for God! So with God, you can take any mountain that God has promised you. By His authority, you can drive out any giants that stand in your way.

Take your mountain in God! Possess what belongs to you in Christ!

Prayer:

Lord, give me this mountain of _____ (describe what you desire from God.)

Lord, I realize I've backed away from this mountain in the past. But today I come to You with a determination to take my inheritance in Christ by the Spirit of God, not by the force of my own might.

As I work together with Your Spirit and Your Word, I shall overcome the giants and hindrances that would try to oppose me. And I shall stand on the crest of that mountain, victorious through Your Spirit and Your Word.

Thank You, Father, for my promised land. It's mine! Faith says I have it now! I thank You for my possession in Christ in the Name of Jesus."

Chapter 4
Faith Takes Possession Of God's Promise

Joshua was now the leader of the Israelites, and for the second time the Israelites stood surveying their Promised Land. The generation of Israelites who had rebelled against the Lord had died in the wilderness just like the Lord said they would.

The younger Israelites had grown up, and they were finally ready to cross over the Jordan River to possess their Promised Land. All the promises God made to the children of Israel forty years before were about to come to pass.

In all those forty years of wandering in the wilderness with those rebellious Israelites, Joshua and Caleb never once quit believing God. Certainly their faith had been tried and tested as they wandered forty years with those unbelieving Israelites. But they never gave up their faith in God because they knew that with God, they could take the land.

Penetrating Impossible Barriers

God told Joshua to command all the people to cross over the Jordan River and possess the Promised Land. Caleb and Joshua had wholly followed the Lord in their hearts and in their speech, so they were ready to obey

God, no matter what He commanded.

JOSHUA 1:1-11
1 Now after the death of Moses the servant of the Lord it came to pass, that the Lord spake unto Joshua the son of Nun, Moses' minister, saying,
2 Moses my servant is dead; now therefore ARISE, GO OVER THIS JORDAN, thou, and all this people, UNTO THE LAND WHICH I DO GIVE TO THEM, even to the children of Israel.
3 Every place that the sole of your foot shall tread upon, that have I given unto you, as I said unto Moses.
4 From the wilderness and this Lebanon even unto the great river, the river Euphrates, all the land of the Hittites, and unto the great sea toward the going down of the sun, shall be your coast.
5 There shall not any man be able to stand before thee all the days of thy life: as I was with Moses, so I will be with thee: I will not fail thee, nor forsake thee.
6 Be strong and of a good courage: FOR UNTO THIS PEOPLE SHALT THOU DIVIDE FOR AN INHERITANCE THE LAND, which I sware unto their fathers to give them.
7 Only be thou strong and very courageous, that thou mayest observe to do according to all the law, which Moses my servant commanded thee: turn not from it to the right hand or to the left, that thou mayest prosper whithersoever thou goest.
8 This book of the law shall not depart out of thy mouth; but thou shalt meditate therein day and night, that thou mayest observe to do according to all that is written therein: for then thou shalt make thy way prosperous, and then thou shalt have good success.
9 Have not I commanded thee? Be strong and of a good courage; be not afraid, neither be thou dis-

> mayed: for the Lord thy God is with thee whither-
> soever thou goest.
> 10 "Then Joshua commanded the officers of the
> people, saying,
> 11 Pass through the host, and command the peo-
> ple, saying, Prepare you victuals; for within three
> days YE SHALL PASS OVER THIS JORDAN, to go
> in to possess the land, which the Lord your God
> giveth you to possess it.

When God told the Israelites to go in and possess their land, the only problem was that the Jordan River lay as an impenetrable barrier between them and the land of promise. The river was at flood stage, and there was no way to cross it!

God knew the Jordan River was there when He told them to cross over to their Promised Land. But still He gave the command to Joshua: *". . . arise, GO OVER THIS JORDAN, thou, and all this people, unto the land which I do give to them. . . ."*

How did He expect the Israelites to get across that river? Isn't it interesting that just because they ran into an impossibility, God didn't tell them they could quit. That impossible barrier didn't seem to bother God!

You see, it didn't make any difference to God that the Jordan River blocked the Israelites' passage into the land. Why? Because impossible barriers are nothing to God!

Once again, God gave His people a plan so that by His strength and wisdom, they could accomplish the impossible.

JOSHUA 3:6-17

6   And Joshua spake unto the priests, saying, Take up the ark of the covenant, and pass over before the people. And they took up the ark of the covenant, and went before the people.

7   And the Lord said unto Joshua, This day will I begin to magnify thee in the sight of all Israel, that they may know that, as I was with Moses, so I will be with thee.

8   And thou shalt command the priests that bear the ark of the covenant, saying, WHEN YE ARE COME TO THE BRINK OF THE WATER OF JORDAN, YE SHALL STAND STILL IN JORDAN.

9   And Joshua said unto the children of Israel, Come hither, and hear the words of the Lord your God.

10 And Joshua said, Hereby ye shall know that the living God is among you, and that he will without fail drive out from before you the Canaanites, and the Hittites, and the Hivites, and the Perizzites, and the Girgashites, and the Amorites, and the Jebusites.

11 Behold, the ark of the covenant of the Lord of all the earth passeth over before you into Jordan.

12 Now therefore take you twelve men out of the tribes of Israel, out of every tribe a man.

13 And it shall come to pass, AS SOON AS THE SOLES OF THE FEET OF THE PRIESTS that bear the ark of the Lord, the Lord of all the earth, SHALL REST IN THE WATERS OF JORDAN, that the waters of Jordan shall be cut off from the waters that come down from above; and THEY SHALL STAND UPON AN HEAP.

14 And it came to pass, when the people removed from their tents, to pass over Jordan, and the priests bearing the ark of the covenant before the people;

15 And as they that bare the ark were come unto

Jordan, and the feet of the priests that bare the ark were dipped in the brim of the water, (for Jordan overfloweth all his banks all the time of harvest,)
16 That the waters which came down from above STOOD AND ROSE UP UPON AN HEAP very far from the city Adam, that is beside Zaretan: and those that came down toward the sea of the plain, even the salt sea, failed, and were cut off: and THE PEOPLE PASSED OVER right against Jericho.
17 And the priests that bare the ark of the covenant of the Lord stood firm on dry ground in the midst of Jordan, and all the Israelites passed over on dry ground, until all the people were passed clean over Jordan.

The Lord told Joshua to instruct the priests to cross over the Jordan River first, carrying the ark. As soon as the soles of their feet touched the water, the Lord said that the Jordan River would stand up in a heap so all the people could pass over on dry ground.

In the natural, it sure didn't make any sense to send the priests into a river at flood stage. Flood-stage water is always swift water. That's why in our day the news media announces when there are flash-flood warnings. You're never supposed to get into flood water because it's so swift, it will suck you under and consume you!

How many of you have ever felt overwhelmed by the circumstances of life? Sometimes it seems as though circumstances come in like a flood and try to sweep everything around you into its current — including you! And maybe sometimes you feel like you're hanging on for dear life.

So when Joshua gave that command, you can understand why maybe the priests thought, *But, Joshua, the river is swift. We'll be swept away and drowned. What are you trying to do to us!*

But Joshua had heard from the Lord, and he'd seen the Lord's great faithfulness in all the miracles He'd performed forty years before. So Joshua was ready just to obey.

The younger Israelites had also heard the accounts about the miraculous feats God had performed for their fathers coming out of Egypt. The supernatural wonders of God had been passed down by word of mouth to each generation.

The Israelites knew that God had parted the Red Sea so their forefathers could walk over on dry ground. So when Joshua said, "Let's march!" no matter what the priests may have thought, they just obediently marched out into the swift waters of the Jordan River.

I want you to notice something. When the priests got to the edge of that riverbank, they didn't stop and say, "Hey, Joshua! Look at the water. The river is still at flood stage! Nothing's happened, Joshua. I thought the Lord was going to do something!" No, they put some action to their faith and stepped into the water.

I want you to notice something else. Those priests could have just stood on the bank of the Jordan River and demanded, "All right now, Lord! You told us to cross this river, so we believe *You're* going to do something about this water so we won't drown."

If they had just stood there without taking a step of

faith, nothing would have happened. No, they had to take that step of faith and obedience and get into the water! Faith takes action!

That's where some of you are at spiritually. There's a river at flood stage that's come into your life, and it's causing you a lot of problems. But instead of taking a step of faith, you're just standing at the bank crying, "Lord, *You* do something about the river."

God already told *you* to take up the ark and cross the river. The Ark of the Covenant represents the Presence of God. When you're born again, you have the Presence of God living *in* you, and you have God's Word dwelling in your heart.

If you'll just get up and take that first step of obedience, the Word dwelling in you will be a light to your feet, showing you exactly where to take the next step.

And the Holy Spirit inside you will show you how to get across any river at flood stage in your life. But the ark of God's Presence won't do you any good until you step out in faith into the water.

Faith and obedience bring God on the scene! God came through for those priests as soon as they stepped into the water. The Jordan parted so the rest of the Israelites could cross over on dry ground.

I think sometimes God just wants to find out whether or not we're really going to obey Him. Sometimes God is just waiting for us to take that first step of obedience, and then our miracle will unfold before us.

Many times when God tells us to do something, we

just have to start out in simple faith and obedience. Faith in God is trusting Him regardless of the circumstances. Then God will make a way where there is no way. That's the way we possess our promised land. It's with step-by-step obedience.

For example, a lot of times when people are sick, they begin making faith confessions, "The Lord has healed me." It's scriptural to confess that you're healed by His stripes. But once you make a faith confession, begin to do something you couldn't do before. Put some *action* to your faith confession!

Some of you just need to get ahold of the Word of God and get in the water! Then you're going to see something happening in your life. You can stand on the sidelines all you want waiting for God to do something, but the Lord is waiting for *your* obedience.

The Lord promised that He would deliver you out of the midst of all your problems, circumstances, and trials no matter what they may be. But whether Your problems are spiritual, physical, financial, or material, it makes no difference to the Lord! No matter how big the problem or the flood seems to be, He *will* deliver you out of all your flood waters!

But just standing on the edge of obedience with hope and wishful thinking, making confessions of faith won't get you over your river so you can possess your promised land.

Those priests could have stood on the side of the Jordan River and praised and thanked God and shouted and danced all day long. But do you know what? Those waters never would have parted for them, and they never would have gotten to the other side.

Some of you just need to grab ahold of the ark, the Presence of God, that's on the inside of you. Then you need to start speaking the Word of God out of your mouth and get into the water.

Maybe God's only told you *one* thing He wants you to do for Him. Get up and do that. Do the little thing He's told you to do, and then He will tell you what else to do. Some of you just need to get up and get with it, and then God will give you the rest of the picture. That's how you possess your promised land.

> **ISAIAH 43:2**
> 2   When thou PASSEST THROUGH THE WATERS [the flood-waters of life], **I will be with thee; and THROUGH THE RIVERS, they shall not overflow thee: when thou walkest through the fire, thou shalt not be burned; neither shall the flame kindle upon thee.**

Sometimes the rivers of life seem to come plunging down upon us, and they seem to try to suck us underneath and destroy us in their swift current. Sometimes we're left in utter despair wondering whether we should give up and quit, or just exactly what we should do.

But in God, you don't ever need to give up. If you quit, you have nothing to gain. But if you keep on going and keep on standing on God's Word in faith, you have everything to gain.

For example, once you've made your faith confession

based on God's Word, don't ever change it no matter how long it takes for the answer to manifest. It's your responsibility to believe and receive God's Word. It's God's responsibility when your answer comes.

Many believers get discouraged after they've stood on the Word for a while. But just remember, you're not a failure until you refuse to try again. Just because you mess up once is no sign you're a failure. You cannot be branded as a failure until you quit trying.

I don't intend for the devil ever to be able to brand me as a failure, because I will never quit standing on God's Word in faith. When God promised that the waters would not overflow me, that tells me I can't go under for going over! I can't be destroyed; I can only be a victor if I just stay in God.

Just remember, in our walk of faith, God never promised us that the floods of life wouldn't come. He never promised us that we wouldn't have some fiery trials. In fact, this scripture in Isaiah says that the floods and trials will come from time to time in life!

However, God did promise that when the floods of life came, *He* would take us through them all. He promised that they wouldn't overflow us or consume us, and that we wouldn't be scorched by any fiery trial.

God has a solution for dealing with the flood waters of life. In Genesis 6:14, we find out about a man by the name of Noah whom God raised up in his generation to deal with flood waters. God commanded Noah to build an ark because a great flood was coming upon the earth in judgment of sin.

GENESIS 6:14
**14 MAKE THEE AN ARK of gopher wood; rooms
shalt thou make in the ark, and shalt PITCH IT
WITHIN AND WITHOUT WITH PITCH.**

The ark was designed to float on top of the flood
waters. When Noah finished the ark, the earth was consumed by a great flood, and all the inhabitants except
Noah and his family were consumed (Gen. 7:1-10).

We need to understand that the ark is a type of
Christ. The ark was a refuge for God's people from the
judgment that fell on those who refused to accept God.

Some people say, "We know we're in Christ, and one
of these days, we Christians will be rescued and taken
out of this world."

Yes, that's true. But you're in Christ right now if
you're born again! Right now you're in the ark of
safety — the Lord Jesus Christ — and you're not being
judged with the world.

Noah was to pitch the ark or *seal* it within and without (Gen. 6:14). In other words, since the ark was
sealed inside and outside, no water could come into it,
and it could float safely on top of the flood waters.
Therefore, everyone inside the ark that Noah built was
safe and sound.

The pitch kept the water out. The word "pitch" is
the same word used in one place for "atonement" (Lev.
17:11). Jesus our atonement is the "pitch" that keeps
the flood-waters out!

You may be experiencing flood-waters in your life,

but if you're inside the ark of safety — the Lord Jesus Christ — you have been covered and sealed from within and without. The enemy cannot destroy you no matter how hard he tries as long as you stay in the ark.

> **ISAIAH 59:19**
> **19 So shall they fear the name of the Lord from the west, and his glory from the rising of the sun. WHEN THE ENEMY SHALL COME IN LIKE A FLOOD, the Spirit of the Lord shall lift up a standard against him.**

Sometimes the enemy tries to come into our lives like a flood. But when the devil comes after you, raise a standard against him by the Name of the Lord Jesus Christ. The flood waters of life cannot overflow you as long as you stay in the ark of safety.

Because of Jesus, you and I have no reason to be fearful of the enemy when he tries to come against us! Fear will cause us to forget what the Word says. The spirit of fear is bondage, but we don't have to allow fear in our lives because we've been delivered from the devil's bondage.

The enemy will try to flood your life with discouragement. He will try to rip you from the ark of safety with fear and anxiety. But I'm going to tell you right now that the only way you can be taken from the ark of safety is to let go of the Presence of God yourself.

When Satan attacks, it can sometimes feel like he's trying to grab ahold of you and pull you from the ark of safety. But if you will hold on to God's unchanging hands, you will find that God's grip on you will never loosen.

The enemy can tug all he wants to and try to pull you into those murky flood waters below, but as you take God's hand, no weapon formed against you shall prosper (Isa. 54:17). You shall come forth victorious because you have a Savior from the flood — the Lord Jesus Christ Himself!

The Jericho March of Victory

You see, just because God told us to possess our promised land, that doesn't mean it's always going to be easy. That was true for the Israelites too.

Immediately after the Israelites dealt with one impossibility — crossing the Jordan River — they were confronted by another impossible barrier. The city of Jericho loomed before them as a mighty impenetrable fortress.

Jericho was a stronghold of the enemy and a fortress no one had been able to defeat. Many battles and many sieges had been fought at Jericho as enemies tried to conquer it, but no one had ever succeeded.

Jericho was the first battle the Israelites encountered after they crossed the River Jordan to take possession of their Promised Land. It's interesting how God told the Israelites to conquer this city.

Joshua was a fighting man. He knew a lot about warfare and military strategy. But Joshua was also a man of faith. God gave Joshua a battle plan for possessing Jericho that didn't make any sense according to sound military strategy. But because Joshua was a man of faith as well as a military man, he trusted the Lord and followed God's plan exactly.

> **JOSHUA 6:1-5**
> **1   Now Jericho was straitly shut up because of the children of Israel: none went out, and none came in.**
> **2   And the Lord said unto Joshua, See, I have given into thine hand Jericho, and the king thereof, and the mighty men of valour.**
> **3   And ye shall compass the city, all ye men of war, and go round about the city once. Thus shalt thou do six days.**
> **4   And seven priests shall bear before the ark seven trumpets of rams' horns: and the seventh day ye shall compass the city seven times, and the priests shall blow with the trumpets.**
> **5   And it shall come to pass, that when they make a long blast with the ram's horn, and when ye hear the sound of the trumpet, ALL THE PEOPLE SHALL SHOUT WITH A GREAT SHOUT; and THE WALL OF THE CITY SHALL FALL DOWN FLAT, and the people shall ascend up every man straight before him.**

The Lord gave the Israelites a battle plan, all right. The only problem was that the Israelites couldn't use their spears and shields or their bows and arrows! In fact, God told them not to use any weapons at all. In the natural, that doesn't make any sense!

Normally in the Old Testament, when one army wanted to conquer a city, they'd have to battle the enemy for it. But in this fight, the Lord told the Israelites that *He* was going to *give* them the city.

Here was God's plan. The Israelites were supposed to march around the city once each day for six days. Then on the seventh day, the priests were supposed to blow a trumpet as the people shouted with a great shout.

Just by following God's battle plan, the Lord said the walls of Jericho would fall down before them. When you study Old Testament history, you can see how impossible that battle plan was in the natural. For one thing, many of these cities were walled and heavily fortified.

For another thing, what good was a shout going to do? It didn't make any sense that strong fortified walls would fall down just because a bunch of people shouted!

But here God told the children of Israel to take that well-fortified city effortlessly with a shout — because *His* power was in the shout! It was a shout of faith and a shout of victory.

Can you imagine the Commander in Chief of an army telling his troops to go into a battle but forbidding them to fight! I can just imagine the generals getting together over at the Israelite pentagon tent, saying, "Our boss has lost his mind. Joshua's gotten soft since he became a leader."

But some of those Israelites were old enough to remember what had happened by not wholly following God in obedience. So regardless of their *opinion* of God's plan, they just obeyed Joshua without question and began to march around those walls.

Can you imagine what the people of Jericho thought as they looked down from Jericho's walls and saw the Israelites marching around the city for six days without uttering a word! They probably said, "What are those Israelites up to? What do they think they're going to accomplish by walking around Jericho like that?"

In the meantime, the Israelites just continued to march around Jericho, wearing down a big pathway around the city as they marched.

We don't always understand everything God tells us to do. But if we'll just obey Him, we'll live to see the triumph of our obedience.

Overcoming Your Spiritual Jerichos

As the children of Israel went in to possess their Promised Land, God never told them that they wouldn't encounter some Jerichos. But He did tell them that He would give them the battle plan and that He would do their fighting for them.

God didn't promise *you* that you wouldn't encounter some spiritual Jerichos in your life as you live for Christ on this earth. But He did tell you that as you trust His Word, He would conquer every one of your Jerichos for you. And He promised to give you the victory in every circumstance in life.

However, when you come up against your spiritual Jerichos, you've got to have the Word of God in your heart. Without it, marching around that Jericho won't do any good. But with the Word in your heart and in your mouth, you can march around those impossible barriers quoting God's Word, and those walls have to come down!

> Greater is He who is in me than he that's in the world.

I can do all things through Christ who strengthens me.

By His stripes I am healed.

In all things I am more than a conqueror
through Jesus Christ who loves me.

God always promises me the victory in every
circumstance.

No weapon formed against me shall prosper.

All my needs are met according to His riches in
glory through Christ Jesus.

If God is for me who can be against me?

Thanks be to God who always causes me to triumph in Christ.

I shall possess what belongs to me in God!

God's Word will knock down any impenetrable barriers or impossible obstacles in your life. But your responsibility is to quote what God says about the situation. Then
once you've spoken the Word over your situation, you
need to praise Him for the answer because that's faith.

In the New Testament, Mark 11:23 and 24 shows us
how to possess our promised land — our Canaan land
on this earth. For the believer, our Canaan land on this
earth is our inheritance in Christ. We enter into our
promised land by believing the promises of God in our
heart and speaking God's Word by faith.

Every believer on the face of this earth has the ability
to receive the fullness of God's redemptive plan for his
own life. He *can* possess what belongs to him in Christ.

You and I have a choice. We can believe God and go
in and possess what belongs to us. Or we can stay

where we're at in faith and never receive what is rightfully ours. We can live a life of plenty or we can live a life of lack. It's up to us.

Does that mean we will never encounter any opposition? No, of course not. We will have to possess our land even when there are spiritual giants that oppose us.

In the New Testament, we fight a spiritual battle with spiritual giants. We don't fight or wrestle against flesh and blood, but against principalities and powers (Eph. 6:12).

But under the New Covenant, our spiritual giants are *defeated* foes. However, we still have to stand in Jesus' victory over Satan in order to possess the land that belongs to us in Christ.

As we're marching through our promised land, the enemy will throw up one barrier after another to try to oppose us. But that doesn't mean we're supposed to stop marching!

When Jesus Christ the Head of the Church gives me marching orders about possessing something that belongs to me in His Word, I just start marching. If I come up against a spiritual barrier, I just march right up to it and stand there quoting the Word.

Eventually, that barrier has to get out of my way! As I quote the Word, I can begin to hear the wall crack as the Word demolishes it piece by piece. Finally the wall just totally cracks and crumbles under the power of the Word. Then I take off marching again because Jesus already told me, "Go possess the land that belongs to you. It's yours!"

Praise Your Way to Victory!

As the Israelites came up against those Jericho walls on the seventh day, they blew the trumpet and shouted praises. Why did God tell them to shout? Because they were shouting the victory in faith! And it wasn't some puny little yell either!

I get amused at people who praise God like they're afraid someone's going to hear them. The Israelites *wanted* the enemy to hear them. They also wanted *God* to hear them, so they raised their voices to God!

Let God know you're praising Him and that you aren't ashamed of it. The Bible says to make a joyful *noise* before Him (Ps. 98:4). No devil in hell, no circumstance — *nothing* can stand in your way when you learn how to praise God based on His Word.

When you're confronted with your spiritual Jerichos, begin to shout the victory *before* you actually see the victory. That's faith.

But many times what happens is that when some believers come up against a little mole hill, they stub their toe and fall down defeated, crying, "Oh, God!" But the Bible says to count it all joy when you fall into different tests and trials (James 1:2).

So when you come up against an obstacle or a problem — a spiritual Jericho — begin to praise God! An obstacle is another opportunity to experience the power of God in your situation. Instead of complaining about the problem, praise God that He's bigger than any Jericho.

Yes, the Bible says that your adversary, the devil,

walks around like a roaring lion (1 Peter 5:8). But it also says you can overcome him in every situation of life with the Name of Jesus, because Jesus already defeated Satan for you.

God told us that we would have trials, tests, and temptations in this life. But He also said that we are more than conquerors through Christ who loves us (Rom. 8:37). That means it doesn't matter what the enemy throws at us, we are more than victors through Christ.

Besides, Satan doesn't have anything new. He pulls the same old tricks he's always pulled. He just wraps them up in new packages. For example, he still uses the same temptations he tried to use on Jesus. He told Jesus, "Follow me and you can have the world and all the pleasure and fun the world has to offer" (Matt. 4:5-10).

Satan tells us the same thing. But what he doesn't tell us is that *his* fun and excitement turns into disaster and death! Only the Lord Jesus Christ can bring life (John 10:10). And the Lord is the only One who can establish us in peace and security (2 Chron. 20:20).

Do you want those walls that have hindered you to come down? Then begin to shout the triumph of praise to God. Shout praises to God when it looks like everything is black and bleak. *Faith believes, faith trusts; therefore, faith praises.*

Many believers panic when they see obstacles. They get frightened. But why get afraid? We haven't been given the spirit of fear, but of love, power, and a sound mind (2 Tim. 1:7).

A sound mind tells you that in every situation, it is

time to praise the Lord because He's greater than any test or trial. A mind that's *not* sound causes you to panic and wring your hands in despair.

Remember when Paul and Silas were confronted with their spiritual Jericho? They were beaten, thrown in prison, and their feet were put in stocks (Acts 16:22-26). If Paul and Silas had panicked, they never would have received their miracle from God and been set free from the shackles of that prison.

If it had been most of us who were locked up in stocks in that jail with Paul, we probably would have said, "Paul, when you invited me on this missionary trip with you, I thought you said *God* told you to do this. But evidently He didn't, because look at us now!"

That's what many believers think when they find themselves in a test or a trial; they think they aren't in God's will. If God tells them to do something and they run into a Jericho or an insurmountable obstacle, instead of praising God, they begin to murmur and complain. They say, "If God really told me to do this, I wouldn't be in this situation right now."

But tests and trials don't determine the perfect will of God! In fact, sometimes when the devil comes in and tries to stop what you're doing, that's your confirmation God really told you to do it!

But when the adversary comes your way, just begin to stand your ground and praise God. Paul and Silas sang praises at midnight with their backs bleeding and their feet in stocks in the innermost part of that prison (Acts 16:25).

The innermost part of the prison was like being in solitary confinement. There wasn't any light or windows — nothing for comfort. Some scholars even say it was like being in a damp, dark, dirty basement.

So there sat Paul and Silas — wet, dirty, with their feet locked tightly in stocks in a smelly, dark prison. Their backs were bleeding where they'd been beaten, but they sang praises anyway.

Midnight represents the darkest hour of your trial. But the midnight hour also means something else. Midnight means it's the last part of the night and the dawning of a new day.

Yes, it's still dark at midnight, but daylight is soon to break. Just wait a few hours, and the sun will brightly shine once again. If we're faithful to praise and worship God, the sun will always shine again on us even in the midst of the darkest test or trial.

If you'll praise God for the victory in the midst of great tests and trials — sooner or later your midnight hour will change to victory. Just keep on praising God, and it won't be long before the light of the Son of God will shine on your life once again. Those tests and trials must fade away, because light dispels the darkness. Victory comes from praising God!

If you really believe God, you will praise Him in the midst of your spiritual Jerichos and your darkest midnight hour. Praise strengthens your faith. Quote God's Word in faith, take your eyes off the problem, and focus on God in praise. Praise empowers you with the mighty ability of God.

Have you ever seen those race cars on the speedway that are suddenly empowered with a blast of power? Those cars are equipped with a booster switch the driver can turn on for more power. When those race-car drivers turn up the power, those cars take off!

That's what praising God does to your faith. If you've been standing your ground believing God for something, and it looks like the trials of life are about to engulf you, press God's booster switch of praise and watch yourself soar to victory!

If God can use the shouts of the Israelites' praise in the Old Testament to level an entire city wall and the Israelites weren't even born-again, how much more will God move in answer to our praises!

Don't be fooled into thinking the devil will leave you alone in life. No, the devil will try to build obstacles in your life to prevent you from receiving what God's promised you. He will make certain that you run up against spiritual Jerichos. But don't get fearful — just begin to praise God.

What will *you* do when you're confronted with impossible situations? Are you going to question God's faithfulness, or are you going to praise Him and watch Him move in your behalf? What you do when you encounter a spiritual Jericho is your key to success or failure.

If you'll praise God, you'll come out of that trial victoriously. And the sooner you start praising God, the sooner you'll start coming out of that trial!

You know, it's a lot harder to get the devil out of your way once he gets a foothold than it is to prevent him from getting a foothold in the first place. So don't let the devil get an upper hand in your life.

Let me show you what I mean. Maybe you're going along in your Christian walk doing just fine when all of a sudden you begin to feel a little ache in your body and a scratchiness in your throat. But it doesn't amount to much, so you don't pay much attention to it.

However, two days later you have a temperature, and the devil has latched onto you with a good case of a cold and the flu. Then it's harder to get rid of him once he's got a real hold on your body.

How can you prevent him from bringing sickness to your body the next time he shows up? The minute he tries to bring the first symptom, begin to praise God because you've been healed by the stripes of Jesus (Matt. 8:17; 1 Peter 2:24).

Don't give the devil a chance to set up camp in your life at all. Don't give him an opportunity to drive his tent stakes down into your life, because then it will take more effort to pull them out.

That's why you should never give the devil the upper hand in your life. Of course, if he's already found a foothold in your life, you can still obtain the victory over him in that situation. But then it usually takes a greater faith stand and more perseverance. So just don't let him get a foothold in your life in the first place!

When you take your stand against the devil with the Word of God, you can say with assurance, "I cannot fail because the Greater One lives in me."

Those times when it seems to be the blackest and the bleakest in your life are the times when you walk through the valley of the shadow of death. It's the *shadow* of death because you can see the evidence of the enemy's kingdom of destruction all around you.

The devil will try to take you through the valley of the shadow of death with its fiery trials. That's when your faith in God will really be tried and tested.

I know what it's like to have the devil jump on my shoulder and say, "What are you going to do now?" Over the years, he's tried to present me with some great opportunities to fail.

But when he tries to discourage me, I just say, "Mr. Devil, I'm going to believe God and do whatever is possible in the natural realm while I'm believing God in the supernatural realm."

I've had great opportunities to quit when the Jerichos showed up in my life. But instead of quitting, I began to praise God because of the promises God gave me in His Word.

You'll have to learn to believe God in the valley of the shadow of death. Learn to praise Him even in the valleys! When it's dark all around you and you're facing impossibilities — your spiritual Jerichos — and it doesn't look like there's any hope in sight, that's exactly when you need to praise God.

Friend, you need to learn how to praise God even when fear confronts you on every side. Praise God when you're up against spiritual impossibilities, financial impossibilities, or any other kind of impossibilities.

When it looks like you're going under instead of going over, that's when you need to say, "No, you don't, Mr. Devil! In Jesus' Name, I have authority over you."

It's easy to have faith when everything is rosy and the sun is shining brightly. But when the thunder rolls in, the lightning starts flashing, and it's dark all around, that's when you find out if you really have faith in God. When you can praise God when the thunder rolls and the lightning flashes — then you know you trust God!

In the midst of the storm, you know you have faith when you can praise God before you see your victory. No matter how you feel, praise God anyway. Feelings don't have anything to do with faith. I'd rather live by faith than to try to make it on feelings.

Feelings are always changing and getting rearranged. That's why you can't depend on feelings. Feelings will let you down every time. But you *can* depend on God's Word. And God never changes, so your faith can remain stable and fixed when it's based on God's unchanging Word.

Don't Take Sides Against God

Friend, you've either got a big God and a little devil, or you've got a big devil and a little God. I don't know about you, but I serve the God of gods and the Lord of lords! There's no god like my God. He was, He is, and He always will be!

The enemy will try to steal everything he can from you. He'll use every weapon he can to get you out of faith — doubt and unbelief, fear and panic. He used doubt and unbelief to rob the children of Israel of their Promised Land.

The Israelites could have gotten their confession in line with God's Word to them and stayed in faith. After all, they had the promise of God. God had even shown them their land. They could have believed God in their hearts and confessed faith in Him with their mouths.

Don't be like the Israelites who took sides against God. Don't take sides against the Word of God by saying about your situation, "It's impossible." That's not what the Word says.

The Word of God says, ". . . *with God nothing shall be impossible*" (Luke 1:37). Jesus Himself said, ". . . *If thou canst believe, all things are possible to him that believeth*" (Mark 9:23).

You can always locate people and find out whether they are negative or positive by listening to what they say. Negative people always talk about what they *don't* have and what they *can't* do. They focus on how weak they are and what they can't accomplish.

Many people have just allowed their personalities to become negative through wrong thinking. Every time they open their mouth about something, they confess the negative side of life.

For example, if you're a pastor and you've ever tried to start a new building program, you probably know there are always some people who are quick to say, "It can't be done." Sometimes they don't even wait to hear your plan. They just say, "We can't do it because . . ."

Or if you're about to change procedures in your business operation, there are always those who will say, "Oh, it will never work! We've been doing it this way for years. It'll never work any other way!"

Sad to say, sometimes *we* are the ones who say, "We can't! It's impossible!" or "It will never work!" Don't be like the Israelites who perished in the wilderness because they refused to believe God. Stay in faith! Agree with God. No matter what your situation, speak in line with God's Word.

When you speak contrary to God's Word, you hinder God from moving on your behalf. God wants you to possess everything He's promised you. It wasn't God's will that the Israelites wandered in the wilderness forty years and never possessed the land. But they got exactly what they confessed.

If you've been thinking wrong and talking wrong, you'd better ask God's forgiveness! Get your words and your thinking in line with God's Word and begin to talk right. That's one way you begin possessing your promised land. The Israelites learned the hard way not to oppose God. Learn from their mistakes.

Practically speaking, there are two ways to learn hard lessons. You can learn the easy way from someone else's experience, or you can learn the hard way from your own experience.

For example, if you stick your finger in a light bulb socket, you can learn the hard way that you'll get a shock. That's learning by your own experience. Or you can learn by listening to someone who has experience when he warns you, "Don't stick your finger in the light bulb socket!"

I don't know about you, but I'd rather learn the easy way from someone *else's* experience!

When Dad pastored the Farmersville church in Texas years ago, I was about four years old. We lived in a little ole shotgun parsonage. That means you could shoot a gun straight through the house because it didn't have any other rooms to it!

We didn't have any table lamps in those days because we were so poor, but we did have one of those old-fashioned light bulb sockets that just sticks into the wall. There wasn't a switch on it. We just turned the light bulb on or off by screwing it in or unscrewing it.

As a four-year-old, I was playing on the couch in the living room, and I decided to play with that light bulb socket. Dad said to me, "Son, leave that alone. Don't get your finger in there! It will bite you!"

I just tapped around the edges of the socket with my finger for a while, and nothing happened. I kept playing around, poking my finger here and there, and eventually my finger slipped off the edge and made contact right in the center of that socket. The force of that electric shock knocked me over backwards into the middle of the floor.

I got up, and Dad said, "I warned you, didn't I? You wouldn't listen, so you had to learn by experience."

Another time when I was a little older, I did the same thing with an electric fan. Dad told me three times, "Son, leave that fan alone. If you get your finger in there, it will cut you."

Well, I discovered that I could put the fan on low and then turn it off and stop it with my finger. I thought that was fun, so I turned the fan on high and got it going really good. Then I turned it off and stuck my finger in there to stop the blade, and the blade just split my finger wide open.

You see, I chose to learn from my *own* experience, instead of learning from the wisdom of someone *else's* experience. But sometimes that's the way we Christians are with God too! He warns us, but sometimes we just don't listen to Him, so we have to learn the hard way.

The children of Israel's experience was to be an example for us (1 Cor. 10:11). We can learn from *their* experience so we don't have to make the same mistakes. We won't have to pay the same consequences they paid if we'll just obey God.

Those Israelites who believed God crossed over to the other side and claimed what belonged to them. *You* need to cross over to the other side of *your* situation in faith and claim what belongs to you too!

That's why even under the New Covenant, we need to watch our words. God's Word said we are to follow God and keep His statutes. That includes living holy lives before God.

The Bible says that God's Word doesn't return to Him void (Isa. 55:11). So if we're faithful to take Him at His Word, what a harvest it will produce!

For example, in the realm of healing, God's Word said that by Jesus' stripes we *were* healed. If we *were* healed, then we are healed!

So quit going around telling people, "I sure wish God would heal me." All that does is grieve God because He's already paid for your healing through Jesus' redemption at the Cross of Calvary. Healing belongs to you *now*! So let your words agree with God's Word and receive your healing by faith! Rise up and accept what is yours.

Speak the Word Over Your Situation

Believers beg and cry and plead with God to perform wonders for them, but God has already made full provision for them in every area of life through Jesus Christ.

After Jesus rose again from the dead, He said to the Church, "All power and authority has been given unto Me, both in Heaven and in earth" (Matt. 28:18). Then He ascended on High and sat down at the right hand of God the Father.

After Jesus ascended on High, He sent the Holy Spirit to be with His people. And He gave us, the Body of Christ, the power of attorney to use His Name to receive whatever we need.

Jesus also gave us His Word with all those great and mighty promises. And He gave us the Holy Spirit as the power behind His Name to deliver us and set us free.

So it's time we quit talking about what we *don't* have and start talking about what we *do* have! It's time we start talking about what we possess and who we are in Christ. Let's talk about what we can be in Christ because we have the powerful anointing of the Holy Spirit working in us and through us.

It's time that you as a believer begin to speak the Word with authority over your situation. Move out in the power of the Holy Spirit to receive what belongs to you. This day is your day to begin possessing your promised land!

If you haven't believed God in the past and have hung back wallowing in doubt and unbelief instead of charging yourself up with faith, start taking God at His Word. Don't create confusion and havoc by your negative words, because negative words can affect others around you too.

Believe what God says in His Word. God will reward those who diligently seek Him and stand in faith on the integrity of His Word. Look how God rewarded Caleb and Joshua for their diligence. They spoke in faith, and they received what they desired from God.

Friends, you're going to have to stand on God's Word to receive your inheritance in Christ. When you begin to wholly follow God and take Him at His Word, just watch God perform wonders for you!

Sometimes you'll have to stand on God's Word when all the circumstances scream, "It's impossible!" I've had to do that many times, and God's Word has never failed me yet.

For example, in the early '80s, we built several buildings on the RHEMA campus. Four buildings were completed at one time. That means those bills all came due about the same time. If you've ever been involved in a building project, you know what can happen when all the bills come due at once.

The devil kept saying to me, "You're not going to succeed. You're done for!"

When the enemy spoke those words of doubt to me, I jumped up from my desk, and grabbed my Bible. I said to the devil, "Devil, you're a liar and the father of lies. That's what the Bible said about you, and it's true! I refuse to listen to your lies."

I said to the devil, "Devil, do you see this Bible? The Word of God says that all these bills are paid according to His riches in glory!"

Then God gave me a plan for possessing our promised land, which at that time was paying off that building project. I said, "Every day I'm going to sit down at that desk and see how much money we've got. Then I'm going to pay one bill of that amount. And tomorrow when the money comes in, I'm going to pay what I can for that day.

"I'm going to do that every day because I know that God will provide for us every day, and the money will come in to meet our needs. I'm going to do that every day until every bill is paid."

Then I said to Satan, "When the sun comes up two months from now, you're going to be over in the corner like a whipped dog because every bill will be paid, and

God's Word will once again triumph!"

And two months later, the Word proved Satan to be the liar that he is because every bill was paid!

I never told people that their money was in the mail until I actually mailed the check, because that's not speaking *faith* — that's *lying*! But I did act in faith on the Word and stand my ground, and God's Word doesn't fail!

We came through that building project successfully because the Word of God can't fail. The Word always comes through for us and prospers in what it was sent to do.

A Second Battle Plan

I'm going to tell you something else that will help you possess your promised land. When you enter into the good fight of faith by standing on God's Word against the devil's lies, always remember that Satan is a defeated foe (Col. 2:15).

However, it's also important to understand that any good commander always has a second line of defense or a second battle plan. What do I mean by that? I've never seen a military chief go into battle without a second line of attack. Even in sports, you always have a second line of defense.

For example, in football and basketball, the coach designs game plans and strategies. A team may start with one plan. But if the defense doesn't hold up against the opposing team, the coach may switch to another game plan. A second line of defense just demonstrates a team's determination to win.

When you enter into the good fight of faith, you'd better be sure you have a couple of game plans that are in line with God's Word. Then if Satan tries to come against you on another front, you can just turn around and use your second line of defense. You can march on to victory with the Word!

Some years ago, I faced the toughest crisis I've ever faced in my life. Four doctors looked at me and my wife and said, "Your son has a brain tumor. His life is in danger. The tumor is touching the brain stem. One shake of his head, and he's gone.

"It can be removed surgically without any complications or problems. However, anytime the brain is operated on, it's major surgery and there are risks involved."

I talked to Dad, and he said, "In this situation, son, if we don't have an instant manifestation of healing, we'll have to go to a second line of defense or a second plan of attack and use medical science to remove the tumor."

Well, we did not receive an instant manifestation of healing. I prayed and God gave me peace in my heart about going ahead with the surgery. But then the devil began to say, "Here you preach divine healing, and your son is going to have major surgery. What are people going to think?"

But let me show you something about a second plan of attack. If you drop back to a second plan of attack or another faith strategy, you still have to believe God. You still have to confess His Word and stay in faith.

My wife and I finally made the decision that our son would have the brain surgery, because we knew that God can move in the realm of medical science too. So we told the doctors, "Yes, we will go ahead with the surgery."

The doctors said the surgery would last about five or six hours once they opened Craig's skull.

A couple of nurses who had followed our ministry for many years visited Craig the night before the surgery. The next day, Craig was taken into the surgery room at 7 o'clock that morning, and he came out of the recovery room at 7 o'clock that evening.

After the surgery, one of the nurses who had visited Craig told us, "It was amazing how real the power of God was in that operating room! I've been believing God for healing for my back for some time, and my healing was manifested in the middle of the surgery!"

One of the medical personnel said, "It was a text-book-perfect surgery."

When we took Craig back to the doctor for his final checkup some time after his surgery, the doctor said, "That boy is 100-percent normal. He can play any kind of sports he wants because there isn't a trace of that tumor anywhere! He can even play football."

Then the doctor grabbed my hand, and said, "Let's give God the glory!"

You see, I learned something about a second plan of

attack during that crisis. Of course divine healing is God's best, but it is still scriptural to drop back to a second line of attack. Even with a second plan of attack, you'll still have to stand your ground on the Word. In our case, the doctors warned us that there were risks involved.

But I stood my ground on the Word against the devil's lies and said, "It will be a successful surgery. Craig will be fine." I knew that the Bible says if I say with my mouth what I believe in my heart based on God's Word, I can have what I say.

You need to get God's Word in your heart and start saying what you believe! Maybe you're believing God for something, but you haven't had an instant manifestation yet of your healing or your miracle. Don't give up! Just stay in faith so you can possess what belongs to you.

Divine healing is spiritual healing because it is done by God. And you receive it in your spirit first, before it is manifested in your body. But doctors can help you get well too.

Whether you receive your healing by the Word of God or you believe God's Word to work through medical science — God's Word works! Whether you use the first plan of attack or a second plan of attack — God's Word still works!

You've got to learn to take God at His Word. That's how you possess all the promises of God for your life. You don't have to depend on someone else's faith. If you'll believe God for yourself, God will help you possess your promised land. Nothing is impossible with Him!

Don't Get Too Busy for God

Sometimes we can miss God's best in life because we get too busy with the cares of this life. That's one reason why when we face a crisis, we sometimes have to use a second battle plan of attack.

That's why in my life, I've learned to devote a certain time each day to prayer and reading the Word of God. And if it's my prayer time, I don't care how many phone messages are laying on my desk or how many people are waiting to see me, I read the Word. Everything and everyone waits until I've read the Word and talked to God.

I've learned to do that over the years because without the Word and prayer, we are nothing. It's so important how we talk and what we say, but there's no way we can get our thinking and our talking straightened out unless we spend time in the Word of God. It's that simple.

When our thinking is renewed with the Word and our confession and our lifestyle lines up with the Word, then we can receive from God.

If you want to possess your promised land, you need to purpose in your heart to set aside the cares of this life and spend time alone with God. If you need to take the telephone off the hook, do it!

I remember reading about a famous pastor in England who lived many years ago. This minister instructed his staff never to disturb him during his prayer time.

One day the prime minister of England came to see this pastor. The pastor's young assistant thought the prime minister's visit was important enough to interrupt him.

The young assistant knocked on the door, and said, "Rev. So-and-so, the Prime Minister is waiting to see you."

The minister replied to his young assistant, "Tell him to take a seat; he'll have to wait for me. For the next thirty minutes I've got an audience with the King of kings."

That's the kind of commitment you need to have to fellowship with God so you can possess your promised land. If you've never taken advantage of rich fellowship with the King of kings, go into His Presence today and enjoy an audience with Him.

Fellowship with Him in His Word. Then when you speak, there will be power in your words. That's when the miraculous starts happening in your life!

Take Your Place!

It's time that the Church of the Lord Jesus Christ starts fulfilling all that we are supposed to be on this earth. We are to be a powerful force for God! In order to be full of the power of the Holy Spirit, we have to *believe* what God says and *do* what God says, no matter what we face.

Just remember that God has already given you the land. It's yours *now*. Your inheritance in Christ belongs to you. Don't give up and say, "Well, I *thought* God was going to give me what He promised me. But I guess He's not."

Recognize the enemy as your source of opposition. The devil is the one trying to keep you from receiving from God, not God. God's already given you the land through the Lord Jesus Christ.

Then don't keep your eyes on the enemy — look to the Word of God. You need to begin to march into your promised land using the sword of the Spirit, quoting the Word of God, and singing the praises of God.

You need to march through your land singing God's praises and standing on His promises. When the storms of doubt and fear try to come against you, stand on God's promises and you will prevail!

Sometimes when there's been no way out of impossible situations, I had to tell myself, "God said, 'Possess the land,' so I'm going to do it!" And I've said to the Lord, "Lord, I'm standing on Your Word. I'm standing on Your promises. No devil from hell is going to keep me from receiving what You've promised me, Lord. Your Word says it, I believe it, and that settles it.

When I have God's Word settled in my heart, I can walk away shouting the victory, full of faith. Because God is real and He's faithful to His Word, you can have your victory too. It's up to you.

It's up to you to begin to confess the promises of God about your situation. Begin to meditate on the Word in your heart and speak it with your mouth.

Don't sit around and do nothing about your situation. Speak God's Word over your life and your circumstances. Put God's Word into action in your life by speaking faith-filled words that are based on God's Word.

Make this confession from your heart:

> Heavenly Father, I purpose right now to possess what belongs to me in Christ. Your Word promises me an inheritance in Christ. It's mine. I refuse to let the enemy steal it from me. I see my promised land with the eye of faith.
>
> I stand on Your Word. I stand on the Word that says greater is He who is in me than the devil that is in the world. The devil is a liar. I won't allow him to take what's mine. I'm going to receive everything You have for me in this life.
>
> I am an overcomer in Christ Jesus. All my needs are met according to Your riches in glory through Christ Jesus. I am a victor in Christ. I can do all things through Christ who strengthens me.
>
> I possess now what belongs to me. It's mine. Faith says I have it now. I say it with my mouth because I believe it in my heart. Thank You, Heavenly Father, it's mine!

Chapter 5
Disobedience Can Cost You Your Dreams

The God we serve is an awesome, mighty God. He has at His disposal such a bountiful reservoir of benefits, and He is just waiting to pour out His blessings upon His children — the Body of Christ. But each one of us will have to get in line with His Word so He can richly bless us as He desires.

Obedience to God will help you receive what God has promised you in this life. If God has given you hopes and dreams that will bring Him glory, He wants you to seek Him diligently so He can bring His promises to pass in your life.

Wait before God in prayer and in His Word so He can reveal His plan to you. Then obey Him step by step so He can bring you into your promised land. It's not hard for God to bring His will to pass in your life. But sometimes it seems difficult for us just to take Him at His Word and obey Him.

Obedience is a key to possessing your promised land in this life. Your promised land includes living in the rich benefits of your redemption in Christ — healing, prosperity, and abundance in every area of life.

God is no respecter of person (Acts 10:34). What He's done for one person, He will do for another. It all depends on your obedience and faith to follow Him completely.

Look at the saints of God in the Word. God fulfilled His plan in the lives of those who were obedient. But those who disobeyed God hindered Him from moving fully like He wanted to.

Why Didn't Moses Enter the Promised Land?

For example, near the end of his life, Moses hindered God from fulfilling the plan of God for his life. Yet Moses was God's chosen deliverer. He had been diligent at leading the children of Israel out of the bondage of Egypt.

The Bible even says that Moses was the friend of God (Exod. 33:11). It also says that God knew Moses face to face: *"And there arose not a prophet since in Israel like unto Moses, whom the Lord knew face to face"* (Deut. 34:10).

But have you ever thought about the fact that even though Moses was God's friend and Israel's deliverer, he never possessed the land that he started out journeying toward years before?

He looked at the Promised Land, but he never possessed it. All he ever got to do was stand on a mountaintop and see the land in the distance. Disobedience cost Moses his dreams.

What prevented Moses from possessing his Promised Land? We need to learn from Moses' experience, so we won't make the same mistake he did. If we can learn from his mistake, it will help us successfully possess all that God has for us.

Actually, Moses is a representation of the Law. God gave Moses the Law on Mount Sinai. Moses spent forty days and forty nights in God's Presence, and God wrote on the tablets of stone with His finger (Exod. 31:18). Moses represents the Law, which could not bring the people of God into the Promised Land.

> **ROMANS 8:3,4**
> 3 For WHAT THE LAW COULD NOT DO, in that
> IT WAS WEAK THROUGH THE FLESH, God send-
> ing his own Son in the likeness of sinful flesh, and
> for sin, condemned sin in the flesh:
> 4 That the righteousness of the law might be ful-
> filled in us, who walk not after the flesh, but after
> the Spirit.

Jesus Christ represents grace and truth. Jesus is the representation of what cannot be accomplished through the flesh, but what must be accomplished through the Spirit.

> **JOHN 1:17**
> 17 For the LAW was given by MOSES, but GRACE
> and TRUTH came by JESUS CHRIST.

It will take Jesus Christ, not the Law of Moses, to bring each one of us into our promised land.

But I want you to realize that Moses worked dili-gently for God to deliver the Israelites out of bondage and bring them to their Promised Land. He worked hard to be the godly leader the people needed and to be everything God required him to be.

Yet he never possessed what he worked so hard to

attain. What was the disobedience that cost Moses his
dreams of entering the Promised Land?

> **NUMBERS 27:12-14**
> **12 And the Lord said unto Moses, GET THEE UP
> INTO THIS MOUNT ABARIM, and SEE THE LAND
> which I have given unto the children of Israel.**
> **13 And when thou hast seen it, thou also shalt be
> gathered unto thy people, as Aaron thy brother
> was gathered.**
> **14 For YE REBELLED AGAINST MY COMMAND-
> MENT in the desert of Zin, in the strife of the con-
> gregation, to sanctify me at the water before their
> eyes: that is the water of Meribah in Kadesh in the
> wilderness of Zin.**

Many believers today remind me of Moses as he
looked from that mountaintop surveying the land
before him.

The Bible talks about the exceeding great and precious promises that are given to us in Christ (2 Peter
1:4). Many believers are looking from the mountaintop
of their position in Christ. They see all the benefits they
can possess in Him. But just like Moses who never
entered the Promised Land, many believers don't *take
possession* of all that the Bible promises them.

If there is any mark against believers, it is the fact
that some of them do a lot of *talking* about their inheritance in Christ, but very little *possessing* of what rightfully belongs to them.

I don't mean to be negative. But the fact remains
that in the natural if you talk a lot and never produce
any results, you get a reputation for being a windbag!

One reason many Christians aren't possessing what belongs to them in Christ is that they're trying to do it their own way. They may say, "Oh, yes, I see healing in the Word." Or "I believe prosperity is scriptural!"

But their real attitude is, "I want to possess all the great and precious promises that belong to me, but I want them on my terms. Now, Lord, this is the way I want You to do it . . ."

You may know what belongs to you in Christ, but if you try to dictate to God how He's going to give you your blessings, you won't be able to receive your inheritance! You have to allow God to do *what* He wants to do, *when* He wants to do it.

That was Moses' problem. God told Moses exactly what He wanted him to do, but Moses didn't do it God's way. God told Moses to gather the people of Israel together and *speak* to the rock. Then water would come forth to give to the people.

NUMBERS 20:1-12
1   Then came the children of Israel, even the whole congregation, into the desert of Zin. . . .
2   And there was no water for the congregation: and they gathered themselves together against Moses and against Aaron.
3   And the people chode with Moses, and spake, saying, Would God that we had died when our brethren died before the Lord!
4   And why have ye brought up the congregation of the Lord into this wilderness, that we and our cattle should die there?
5   And wherefore have ye made us to come up out of Egypt, to bring us in unto this evil place? it is

no place of seed, or of figs, or of vines, or of
pomegranates; neither is there any water to drink.
6   And Moses and Aaron went from the presence
of the assembly unto the door of the tabernacle of
the congregation, and they fell upon their faces:
and the glory of the Lord appeared unto them.
7   And THE LORD SPAKE UNTO MOSES, saying,
8   TAKE THE ROD, and gather thou the assembly
together, thou, and Aaron thy brother, and SPEAK
YE UNTO THE ROCK before their eyes; AND IT
SHALL GIVE FORTH HIS WATER, and thou shalt
bring forth to them water out of the rock: so thou
shalt give the congregation and their beasts drink.
9   And Moses took the rod from before the Lord,
as he commanded him.
10 And Moses and Aaron gathered the congregation together before the rock, and he said unto
them, HEAR NOW, YE REBELS; MUST WE FETCH
YOU WATER OUT OF THIS ROCK?
11 And Moses lifted up his hand, and WITH HIS
ROD HE SMOTE THE ROCK TWICE: and the
water came out abundantly, and the congregation
drank, and their beasts also.
12 And the Lord spake unto Moses and Aaron,
BECAUSE YE BELIEVED ME NOT, to sanctify me
in the eyes of the children of Israel, THEREFORE
YE SHALL NOT BRING THIS CONGREGATION
INTO THE LAND WHICH I HAVE GIVEN THEM.

Moses got water out of the rock, all right, but he
didn't get it the way God told him to do it! God said to
speak to the rock, and instead Moses *struck* the rock in
anger twice. That's disobedience!

Disobedience is why Moses never possessed what
God had for him. He was still the leader of the
Israelites. He was still God's chosen. But his disobedi-

ence cost him the Promised Land.

How did Moses get into disobedience? At first he did everything just like God commanded him. He took the rod from the Lord, just as the Lord commanded him, and he and Aaron gathered the people together at the rock.

But then look what happened. Moses disobeyed God, and it all started with a wrong *attitude*.

Moses' attitude showed up in what he said. God didn't tell Moses to speak to the *people*; He told him to speak to the *rock*. But, instead, Moses spoke to the people, saying, ". . . *Hear now, ye rebels; MUST WE fetch you water out of this rock? . . .*" (v. 10).

You can see by Moses' statement that he was upset with the Israelites. He was tired of their grumbling and complaining. Every time he turned around, they wanted something else from him or from God. And even after Moses had done so much for them, they were still never satisfied.

They were constantly griping, "Why isn't God doing more for us? Can God prepare a table in the wilderness? Can God give us meat in the wilderness? Why doesn't God give us leeks and onions like we had in Egypt? Come on, Moses! If you're God's chosen, get with it!"

Have you ever noticed that the leader always gets the blame when things go wrong? If the church isn't going well, the pastor always gets the blame.

But I want to tell you a little secret. A church will only be as good as the people sitting in the pews. If the people would really support their pastor, the man in the pulpit could do far more for the people spiritually.

It was that way with Moses. The people blamed Moses for everything that went wrong. But despite the people's rebellious attitude, Moses was still responsible to obey God's instructions exactly.

Because Moses disobeyed, the Lord answered him, "Because you didn't believe Me and respect what I said to you before the Israelites, you won't be the one to bring the congregation into the Promised Land."

Some people think that Moses struck the rock because he wasn't really trusting God and didn't have enough faith just to speak to it. But I believe Moses struck the rock because he was accustomed to using the authority of the rod of God.

After all, when the Israelites were in Egypt, God had told Moses to throw the rod down, and it turned into a snake. Moses picked it up, and it became a rod again in his hand (Exod. 7:10). Moses held that rod over the Red Sea, and the sea parted so the Israelites could walk over on dry ground (Exod. 14:13-31).

So, you see, Moses knew he could trust the authority of the rod of God; it had never failed him before. But this time, that's not what God said to do.

This time, God wanted to do something a little different. He only wanted Moses to *speak* to the rock. But Moses was set in his ways when it came to using the rod of God, and he decided to do it his own way. How many times have we done the same thing!

Moses not only got water out of rock, he got an

abundance of water flowing from the rock. But doing it his way cost him in the long run.

It's the same way with us. We can't do things our own way instead of God's way and expect to prosper. In the long run, our disobedience will always cost us.

Do Things *God's* Way!

If we look at Moses' mistake and what it cost him, we can see why some believers today never inherit what God has promised them — their own promised land — even though it rightfully belongs to them.

Yes, they're saved, and they're God's children. But disobedience has caused them to forfeit their own promised land.

God cannot honor disobedience. You can't possess the exceeding great and precious promises of the Lord Jesus Christ if you persist in doing things *your* own way instead of *God's* way.

If you persist in saying, "This is what I believe! And this is how I'm going to get it!" you may get what you want and then regret it later!

That's what happened to the children of Israel. They always wanted to do things their own way. For instance, they wanted a king. God told them, "I don't want you to have a king because I don't want you to be like other nations. *I* want to be your King. But if you persist, you'll get your king all right — but it will cost you."

But the people persisted in their demands, and finally

God let them have a king, even though He knew it wouldn't be good for them in the long run (1 Sam. 8:5-22).

Many believers today do the same thing. They pray and pray for what they *think* they want and need. But sometimes it would be better for them if God didn't answer some of their prayers in the way *they* want them answered!

When believers' requests aren't in line with God's perfect will for their lives, God knows that if He answers their petition, it will be harmful to them.

Sometimes we act like Moses did when he struck that rock with the rod. We have our own way of doing things. And when God asks us to do things a little differently or to change our program or routine, we get upset and begin to murmur and complain.

But when God says to change and do things differently, it's always for our good. On the other hand, *not* doing it God's way is dangerous!

Besides, we can get into a rut, even in the faith walk by just doing things the same way all the time. That's one reason we need to follow God's direction. But when we know certain faith principles work, we can get stagnant, thinking, *Well, God is going to answer my prayer this way every time.*

We fail to realize that God is a God of diversity. God doesn't necessarily do everything the same way every time. He always works in line with His Word, but He may answer our prayer differently than we thought He would.

But whether or not we understand how God is going to answer our prayers, we'll do ourselves a favor by just obeying Him. God is not limited. He has many ways of doing things.

For example, we can even get into a rut in our church services when we do the same things the same way Sunday after Sunday. We can get into a routine that doesn't give the Holy Spirit any room to move.

For instance, some churches sing the same songs the same way every time. Or if the Spirit of God begins to move one Sunday while the congregation is singing a certain song, some people want to sing that same song the same way the *next* Sunday. They think that's how to get the Spirit of God to move and demonstrate Himself!

But if we try to put the Holy Spirit in a box like that, we can actually *quench* the move of God in our services. Doing things our own way *always* costs!

You can't *make* the Holy Spirit move in a church congregation! Actually, thinking *we* can get the Holy Spirit to move puts all the attention on *us* — on what *we* can do and on our own efforts. But the attention shouldn't be on us — it should be on *God*. Let's just let God be God!

Really, that's where Moses went wrong. By speaking to the people and striking that rock twice with the rod, he called attention to himself. He was showing the people what *he* could do.

When Moses said, "All right, you rebels. *We* are going to give you some water. Here it is!" he totally drew the people's attention away from God to focus on what *he* could produce. And by putting the attention on what *he* could do, he forfeited the privilege to go into the Promised Land.

There's a lesson in that for us! We'd better be sure *God* is the focus of attention and that He gets all the credit and glory — not us!

I wonder what Moses thought about as he stood on that mountaintop looking out over that vast land stretching far off into the distance. The mountain he stood on was Mount Nebo, which represented the regions beyond.

As Moses surveyed the Promised Land, he saw the regions beyond, which God had promised him and the Israelites. He probably had thoughts of regret for his disobedience. Yet he also knew that God was a just God. It wasn't God's fault that Moses didn't enter the Promised Land. Moses' own disobedience had cost him his dreams.

Wrong Attitudes and Motives Can Cost *You* Your Dreams

Many of us are standing today on our mountaintop — our position of joint-seating with Christ (Rom. 8:17). And we are viewing the regions beyond, which include all of our possessions in Christ.

We've seen what God has promised us in His Word. But some of us won't be able to possess what already belongs to us until we check up on ourselves and get in line with God in every area of our lives. Let's make sure we're not in disobedience, even in our attitudes like Moses was.

People don't realize it, but they cut off their own blessings when their attitudes aren't right. Sometimes even though they're obeying God *outwardly*, they forget that God looks on the *heart* of man and sees his attitudes (1 Sam. 16:7).

Wrong attitudes hinder believers more than they realize from being able to receive from God. Sometimes the wrong attitudes are thoughts of jealousy and envy.

For example, many believers today grumble and complain when others get blessed or promoted instead of rejoicing with them. They complain, "Lord, how come they got blessed, and I didn't? I've been believing You longer than they have, and I haven't got my blessing yet!"

I'll give you another example of people who do things for the wrong motive. Some people want certain positions in the church so other people will look up to them and give them honor. They want people to notice them and think they're someone special, instead of just wanting to further the gospel of Jesus Christ.

And if another church member is asked to do something special like lead the church worship service, some people get huffy, wondering why *they* weren't chosen. They say, "Well, bless God! I don't know why *I* wasn't asked to lead the worship service! I could do a better job than *he* can!"

Or if someone resigns as a Sunday school teacher, and another person is chosen to take his place, there's usually always someone who says, "Why wasn't I chosen! I've been just as faithful as he's been!"

People with wrong attitudes like that demonstrate why they weren't chosen! If people only realized that attitudes determine how far you go with God. Attitude adjustments allow you to receive the blessings of God.

God promotes those whose attitudes and motives are pure. So rejoice with others when God blesses them, knowing that the same faithful God who met their need and promoted them will faithfully meet your need and promote you when you're mature enough to handle it.

Many believers want a ministry. But if you could see the real motive of their heart, you'd see that many times the only reason they want a ministry is so that they can enjoy all the bright lights and attention of standing in a pulpit ministry!

And some people want a big ministry overnight. They're not interested in getting people saved, healed, and delivered. They're not interested in helping fellow believers. They're only interested in people knowing who they are.

People like that don't have pure motives before God. And if they don't adjust their motives, it will cost them moving on with God. Until they get their heart right, God won't be able to promote them the way He wants to.

A self-seeking attitude will eventually destroy a person's dreams. The Bible says if *Jesus* is lifted up, He'll draw all men unto *Him*. He didn't say if we lift our ministries up, He'd draw all men unto *us*!

When you try to receive glory to yourself, you also cause others to look to you instead of to God. For instance, in religious circles, sometimes it seems like we've gotten into hero worship of men, instead of worshipping God. And if our man of the hour falls, then we fall with him. That's not right!

Yes, it takes human beings to preach the gospel. But, friend, you have to base your salvation and everything you do on the solid Rock — the Lord Jesus Christ. Only then will you be able to possess everything God has for you.

Then it doesn't matter what happens around you or how many fall or rise or get sideways, crossways, upside down, or any other way! You know *you* can stand firm on Jesus Christ the Rock.

You'll be so secure in your relationship with Jesus that you can receive from Him whatever you need. But you'll have to do it *God's* way and keep your heart attitudes pure.

Why Aren't Believers Possessing Their Promised Land?

Why aren't more believers possessing what belongs to them in Christ? Are they completely trusting God, or is there hidden disobedience somewhere? Do attitudes of wanting to do things their own way hinder God from moving in their lives?

Many believers continually make their faith confessions, stating what they want to possess from God.

They say, "The Word of God says it's mine, so I claim it!"

But with all their faith confessions, are they really possessing their promised land? And if they aren't, why aren't they?

If people will be honest and check up on themselves, they'll usually find disobedience somewhere that's hindered the promises of God from being fulfilled in their lives. And instead of helping the matter, they compound the problem. Then they get into more sin by complaining.

Disobedience is sin. Murmuring and complaining is sin. People like to categorize sin as *little* sins and *big* sins because it makes them feel better about what they're doing. Then they think they can excuse and justify themselves by saying that their grumbling and complaining is just a little, bitty sin.

But sin is sin. And sin will keep you from receiving your promised land. Disobedience can cost you your dreams. In fact, God has some pretty strong things to say about people in rebellion and disobedience. He says, ". . . *rebellion is as the sin of witchcraft* . . ." (1 Sam. 15:23).

Grumbling and complaining usually indicates hidden heart attitudes that need to be adjusted! Maybe believers who can't seem to possess what belongs to them have an attitude problem like Moses did when he struck the rock.

Maybe Moses thought he was just trying to help God out. He might have even thought he was doing God a favor by fulfilling God's commandment his own way.

Many times we're like that too. We pray and ask God for something, and then we think we've got to help Him out to get our answer. For example, if we pray and ask God for finances to meet a particular need, sometimes we try to help God give us the money we need.

I've actually known Christians who did just that. For instance, I knew a fellow who belonged to a prayer group, and he just "happened" to kneel beside a wealthy fellow to pray. Then he began to pray out loud, "Oh, God! You know I'm believing You for money to pay my bills! Oh, God!"

The wealthy man beside him felt sorry for the man and gave him some money, but *God* didn't have anything to do with it! The wealthy man just had a good heart and helped the poor fellow out.

If we're going to believe God to meet a need, let's believe God and not go out and broadcast it, trying to help God out!

Now in certain situations there's nothing wrong with letting people know your need. For example, if your church has an outreach for meeting people's material needs, there's nothing wrong with taking advantage of what's been provided for you.

Sometimes we can be in disobedience to God when we don't take advantage of what God has already provided for us. We pray and God meets our needs, but if it doesn't happen just exactly like we thought it would, we refuse it. But it's nothing but pride if we can't accept God's provision.

You can't dictate to God how He should answer your

prayers or meet your need. Actually, the Word of God says God heard us before we called, so He's already made every provision for us ahead of time.

Sometimes when people don't immediately receive the answer to their prayers, they try to figure out in their own minds why they didn't receive their petition. But if they're not careful, they can lean to their own understanding and end up believing that the Word is not for us today.

Many believers today get mad at God when their prayers aren't answered right away. But they don't have any right to get mad at Him! If their prayers aren't answered, it's not God's fault because God's ways are perfect.

Look at Moses' reaction to God's judgment, and see how Moses responded when God told him that he'd never enter the Promised Land. It's important because it shows us that Moses made an attitude adjustment.

> **NUMBERS 27:15-18**
> 15 And Moses spake unto the Lord, saying,
> 16 Let the Lord, the God of the spirits of all flesh, set a man over the congregation,
> 17 Which may go out before them, and which may go in before them, and which may lead them out, and which may bring them in; that the congregation of the Lord be not as sheep which have no shepherd.
> 18 And the Lord said unto Moses, Take thee Joshua the son of Nun, a man in whom is the spirit, and lay thine hand upon him.

Moses' immediate reaction to God's judgment

showed his godly character. The Bible says Moses was the meekest man on the face of the earth (Num. 12:3).

When God rebuked Moses, Moses didn't even think about himself. His first reaction was selfless; he only thought about the Israelites. He immediately began talking to God about his successor (v.16).

Moses didn't whine and complain and get mad at God, as many of us would have done. He accepted what God told him. After all, it wasn't God's fault; it was his own fault.

God could have said to Moses, "Look, Moses, it's not My fault you lost your inheritance. I told you what to do, but you didn't do it. Therefore, because you failed to obey Me, there's no way I can allow you to possess the Promised Land."

Disobedience will cause *you* to forfeit your promised land and your God-given dreams. On the other hand, the devil will also try to push this principle too far, and get you in a ditch. He'll try to get you to think you don't deserve *anything* because you've made mistakes in the past.

God doesn't want us to get into guilt and condemnation. He wants us to recognize where we missed it, repent and ask His forgiveness, and go on. But unless we ask forgiveness for our disobedience, God cannot allow us to receive certain benefits we're believing Him for.

To successfully take our promised land, we must walk in God's forgiveness and be washed in the blood of the Lord Jesus Christ. And we must stand tall in the

victory Jesus Christ provided for us by wearing the hel-
met of salvation, holding high the shield of faith, and
using the sword of the Spirit — the Word of God — as
we obey God's will for our lives.

Get God's Plan *and* His Timing

Obedience means following *God's* plan for our lives
instead of doing things our own way. We don't need to
know what everyone else is doing in the Kingdom of
God so we can copy them.

We just need to know what God is telling us to do.
Then we need to do it! If Jesus Christ is the motivation
for everything we do, we will be successful.

For example, if God told me to preach the gospel
from the housetops, I'd do it, and I wouldn't care what
anyone thought either! But I'm not going to do something just because someone else is doing it.

And I'm not going to follow someone's else's far-
fetched plans to try to be successful either. I just want
to be sure I receive the plan for my life and ministry
from the Lord Jesus Christ, the Head of the Church.

Get on your face before God and find out what God
wants for *your* life. You don't have to think up your own
plans for your life. Let *God* do it. Besides, He already
has a perfect plan prepared for your life.

If you'll walk closely to Him, God will reveal His
plan to you. But don't try to make His plan happen by
yourself. You couldn't make it happen anyway. If you
could have brought something to pass on your own, you

would have done it long ago.

Many Christians make the mistake of trying to make their promised land happen by themselves or in their own timing. For example, sometimes they can tell there's a change coming in their lives spiritually.

But when they get a little tickle of God's future plans for them, they jump up and run, trying to perform it themselves. Usually, they don't even know where they're supposed to run to.

That's one reason some believers aren't possessing anything. They're just out there running. They don't know where they came from, where they're going, or what to do when they get there!

Just stay put until you know you've heard from God *and* you know His timing. Then do *what* God says to do *when* He says to do it. Then you'll begin possessing what He's promised you.

Don't be concerned about how you're going to hear from God. Just check up on yourself. Make sure you're in obedience in every area of life. Make sure you have no hidden attitudes that could keep you from receiving what God has for you. Then trust Him fully. Get in His Word, so God can speak to your heart by His Spirit through His Word.

Once you've received God's instructions, go do what He's told you to do. Determine to follow *His* plan and not your own. You'll find yourself possessing those exceeding great and precious promises that belong to you in Christ.

Do things *your* way and lose. Do things *God's* way and possess what belongs to you in Christ. It's that simple!

It's up to you. It's not up to God. God has already made every provision for you to be a success in life both naturally and spiritually. It's all contained in His Word.

Yes, He'll work with you by His Spirit. But, really, it's up to you whether or not you are a success in this life. Your success depends on your obedience to God and your obedience to His Word.

Many of you are looking for the Holy Spirit to move in some dramatic way so you can receive the promises of God. You think if God moved in a spectacular way in your life, then you could be a success.

But God doesn't move spectacularly by His Spirit in every situation. It's as the Holy Spirit wills (1 Cor. 12:11). However, His Word *always* works, and His Word is supernatural too.

If you're faithful to put the Word of God to work in your life, the Word will work for you. It's not your job to make the promises of God come to pass in your life or to cause God's plan to happen. But it *is* your responsibility to believe God, live right, and stay in faith.

We're totally dependent on God and His Word to perform what He has promised. But your answers are all found in the Book — the Word of God. Obey the Word, and you'll start possessing all the things your heart desires.

If you don't put the Word to work in your life, spiritually you'll be up and down like a rollercoaster. But if you establish yourself in the Word, you'll develop consistency in your life. You'll learn how to consistently possess the exceeding great and precious promises of God. It's up to you!

Don't Just Window Shop In the Promised Land!

Friends, I don't know about you, but I don't want to just look at my promised land, but never possess it. That's why each one of us needs to check up on our Christian walk and make sure we don't end up like Moses — just looking and longing, but never possessing what God promised us.

Years ago when my wife and I were just getting started in the ministry, we didn't have any money left at the end of the month, so we could only go window shopping.

But it sure was a great day when I not only looked in the store window and saw something I wanted, but I walked right into that store and took possession of it!

That's what you're supposed to do with the promises of God! Don't just look at them! You don't have to yearn for what already belongs to you. Just take possession of God's promises! Use the God-kind of faith to receive what is yours. They belong to *you* because of your inheritance in Christ.

I don't want to window shop for the things of God. I want to go right in and take possession of what already belongs to me in Christ!

How about you? Do want to window shop in your promised land? Or do you want to just go boldly into the land and possess what is legally yours in Christ?

The Spirit of God will show you how to stand on God's Word for what you need. You can quit just looking and longing for what belongs to you and start possessing the promises of God in every circumstance.

You have the option whether or not you will receive from God. You *can* possess everything God has promised you in Christ. You don't have to wait until you get to Heaven because you have an inheritance in Christ *now*!

As a believer, you've been equipped with the ability to receive what you need from God. God's given you the same measure of faith He's given every believer (Rom. 12:3).

With that measure of faith, you can receive all the promises of God's Word, including provisions for healing, health, joy, and prosperity.

God has given you every promise that pertains to life and godliness (2 Peter 1:3). Now what are you going to do with them? It's up to you.

God already told you in His Word that He would fight your battles for you. The Word said that the battle is not yours, but it belongs to the Lord (2 Chron. 20:17). In the midst of the battle, know that the Lord is working things out for you.

But remember that the Word also warns you that the devil goes about as a roaring lion seeking whom he may devour (1 Peter 5:8). Satan will try to devour you and get you to doubt God. That doesn't mean you have to allow him to!

But if you get into disobedience or start talking doubt and unbelief, you will open a door to the devil. Doubt and unbelief announce to the devil, "Come on in, Mr. Devil. Have a heyday in my life!"

Sin in your life does the same thing. You can allow the devil to hang around you by what you say and do! Don't allow him to hang around you at all!

Sometimes Christians just halfheartedly say to the devil, "All right, devil, I rebuke you. . . ," and then keep right on living in disobedience. The devil doesn't pay any more attention to that than if they'd said, "Jack and Jill went up the hill."

But when you're living according to the Word, you can get bold with the devil, and demand that he leave you alone in the Name of Jesus. Jesus already whipped him, and you put him on the run with the Name of Jesus.

God's Blessings Are Yours —
If You Just Obey!

God didn't leave you without help or comfort in this life. The Lord Himself promised to give you grace in every situation. His grace is sufficient to sustain you through every problem and trial. And He also promised you the victory in every situation (1 Cor 15:57).

In fact, everything you'll ever need to sustain you

and make you a success in this life has been provided for you in your covenant with God.

For example, the Word of God has already told you that by His stripes you are healed. It doesn't say you are *going to be* healed. It says you are *already* healed (Matt 8:17; 1 Peter 2:24)!

The Word also promises that God shall supply all of your needs according to His riches in glory (Phil. 4:19).

God said to the children of Israel: "I'm going to bring you into a land. I will put you in that land and establish you there. If you will obey Me, you shall be an established people of God, and all the people of the world shall look at you and know that you are *My* people."

Under the New Covenant, we are also God's children. We are born-again sons and daughters of God. You and I are a part of the Body of Christ, the Church of the Lord Jesus Christ.

God has already told us, "I'm going to give you the good of the land. If you'll just obey Me, My blessings will overtake you."

Therefore, it's up to you whether or not you possess your promised land. It all hinges on your faith and obedience to God and to His Word. Without faith and obedience, you'll never possess what God has promised you.

Why? Because when you can't see the sun because of the storm clouds of life, you'll need faith to know that God's Word is true. You'll need to know that as you obey Him, He will move mountains on your behalf. When you can't see the answer because the storms of life rage round about you, you'll need faith in God.

When it looks like your ship on life's sea is about to be tossed upside down, you'll need faith to stand firm on the Word of God.

It will take faith in God to declare in the midst of turmoil: "No matter what the devil says or does, I shall prevail because I'm standing on the promises of God. And by faith in God, I will overcome! By faith I will possess the land!"

You can possess your God-given dreams through the Lord Jesus Christ! It's up to you. It's not up to God or anyone else. You can possess what you need in this life to make you a success in God.

Right now, if all you seem to have is lack in your life, it may be that you just have some adjustments to make so you can wholly follow God in every area of your life. Or it may be you just haven't taken ahold of what belongs to you in the Word.

Yes, it takes obedience and faith in God's Word to possess what God has provided for you. So get in line with the Word! Then reach out by faith and receive what is yours.

You can have defeat or failure in life, or you can have joy and success in God. It's up to you. Don't stand gazing afar off at your dreams, just window shopping at the promises of God! Determine to be totally obedient to God. Do whatever He tells you to do.

Then take each promise that belongs to you and

begin to declare your inheritance in Christ. Boldly speak your faith: "As for me and my house, we are going to possess our inheritance!" Come boldly into your promised land and possess what is yours in Christ!

Chapter 6
Faith Fight or Faith Fizzle?

Fight the good fight of faith. . . .

— 1 Timothy 6:12

The Bible gives us a lot of instruction about how we can possess all the promises of God in our lives today. God wants each one of us to possess everything He has for us. He wants to teach us how to fight the good fight of faith using His Word, so our faith won't fizzle out.

Possessing all of God's promises means to receive our inheritance in Christ — our own personal promised land. It means to possess all the promises in God's Word, including those He's personally made to each one of us.

All the Scriptures in God's Word are given to us so we can be molded into the likeness of our Creator. In the Word of God, we find in Christ the image of what we are supposed to be and what we are to possess in Him.

We need to equip ourselves with the Word of God and prepare ourselves by the power of the Holy Spirit. Then fully equipped and prepared, the Holy Spirit will give us *God's* specific plan for receiving our own personal promised land. It will include everything God has for us in His Word. But it will also include specific instructions for each one of us to carry out God's plan to His glory.

177

But sometimes it will take a fight of faith to receive what God has for you in this life. Sad to say, fighting the good fight of faith for your promised land without getting God's plan can result not only in the loss of the battle, but it can also result in the loss of the fight.

If you don't know what God's plan is for you to possess your land, your good fight of faith can end in utter destruction and defeat.

Remember that when the Israelites came to the border of the Promised Land, God gave Moses a plan for taking the land. God knew exactly how He was going to fight the Israelites' battle for them so they could go in and possess what belonged to them.

But then the Israelites got into doubt and unbelief and ended up wandering in the wilderness for forty years. So God had to raise up a new generation of Israelites who would believe Him and take Him at His Word. God is looking for those who will take Him at His Word in our day too!

God in His patience waited for those younger Israelites to grow up, and then He again took them to the border of the Promised Land, and said, "Now go in and possess what belongs to you."

He gave Joshua the plan for possessing the land, and this time the Israelites were obedient to carry out God's plan. They crossed over into the land in spite of a raging river at flood stage and the impenetrable enemy fortress of Jericho. There's always a way when God gives *His* plan!

Get God's Plan

You see, many people get excited about the promises of God to them.

They go out in faith to possess what God has promised them — their own personal promised land — but many of them end up in defeat because their faith fizzles out. They perish for lack of knowledge because they didn't really have a plan — *God's* plan.

You can't receive your promised land from the Lord just by saying, "I'm going to possess the land! I'm going to receive what God has promised me." That's the right *attitude*, but then you've got to get the right *plan*.

In the natural, what happens without a plan? For example, if you were going to start on a long trip from your hometown across the country to Washington, D.C., you'd need a plan. You'd need to find out what road to travel and how long it would take you to reach your destination.

You can't just get out on the highway and start driving if you ever want to arrive at your destination! If you just drove randomly, you're liable to end up just about anywhere.

But some people do that when it comes to possessing their promised land — their inheritance in Christ and the promises of God for their lives. They've found out what God has made available to them in His Word, and they've discovered they have an inheritance in Christ. They want to appropriate what belongs to them in Christ, but they aren't always sure how to do that.

So some believers just jump out into somewhere —
anywhere — and try to do something in their own
strength. All they know is that their personal inheritance in Christ is part of God's redemption. But they
don't know how to receive what belongs to them, so
often they end up in utter chaos.

And that's the reason some people who get started
operating by faith in God's Word experience all kinds of
problems and their faith eventually fizzles out.

They jumped out to do what God told them to do,
but they don't wait before God in prayer for a plan of
action, so they fail before they get started! They didn't
know where they were going when they started, so
when it was all over, they didn't arrive anywhere!

There's a saying in the world that it doesn't matter
whether you win or lose — it's how you play the game.
But that's not true when it comes to the game of life.

In life, it's not just how you play the game that's
important. You must be determined to win. As a Christian, winning is finishing your course with joy because
you've done what God told you to do!

I don't know about you, but I'm not interested in
anything except winning for God. One reason some people don't want to get saved is that all they've ever seen
from some Christians is failure.

In the game of life, your success to God's glory is
important. And in God's sight, winning and finishing
your spiritual course is success.

You won't be able to finish your own course in victory if you come in second place. But in Christ, you don't have to settle for second best. And if you quit in the middle of your spiritual race, you sure won't come in first place!

People who give up never know the joy and the thrill of victory. All they ever know is the agony of defeat. There's no way a person can possess what God has promised him if he quits!

You can start out fighting the good fight of faith to possess God's promises. But if you don't get God's plan of action, your faith can end up fizzling out, or worse yet, perishing. Faith that perishes is faith that fails in the tests and trails of life.

But when you know how to tap into the power and the plan of God by standing in faith on His Word, there's no such thing as *perishing* — there's only *possessing*. Standing in faith on God's Word is how you fight the good fight of faith. In Christ we are more than conquerors because God's Word puts us over!

The Good Fight of Faith

However, you need to know that the enemy is not going to let you possess anything in God without a faith fight. Even the Israelites had to march around the walls of Jericho and shout the victory *in faith* before those walls came tumbling down (Joshua 6:5).

Some believers have the idea that they'll never have a battle, they'll never have a struggle, and they'll never have any problems in life. But they are mistaken!

The devil will try to take every inch of your promised land away from you — if you'll let him! You'll have to fight by faith each step of the way for what rightfully belongs to you. Your fight will only be by faith in God's Word, not by faith in your own strength or ability.

No one is going to float through life winning great victories for God, just by saying, "Glory, glory, hallelujah! Isn't life great!" That idea came out of someone's fairytale book! Actually, it was probably inspired and authored by Satan himself to keep Christians from pressing on in God to take what belongs to them in Christ.

But when we really find out what God's Word has to say about who we are in Christ, then we are ready for the fight of faith. The scriptural way to do battle is to fight the good fight of faith. You do that by declaring God's Word over your situation instead of looking at your circumstances. You take God at His Word.

The greatest weapon you possess to fight the good fight of faith is the Word of God. In fact, the Word is the *only* weapon you need to fight with, backed by the Name of Jesus and the blood of the Lamb (Rev. 12:11).

If you're going to be a possessor of the land — your personal inheritance in Christ — you're going to have to do some standing in faith. And you'll have to get up and put some action to your words. You've got to fight the good fight of faith with knowledge by understanding the principles of God's Word.

Many believers don't know how to enter into the good fight of faith like they should because they don't understand their rights and privileges in Christ. Although they may possess some knowledge, they don't know how to stand in faith on God's Word.

However, this Christian walk sometimes involves a faith fight. It's true that Satan is a defeated foe, but we enforce his defeat in our lives by standing on God's Word and by putting the devil in his place in every circumstance!

You see, the greatest battles that have ever been fought in this life are not the battles that have been fought in the air, on land, or at sea. No, the greatest battles that have been fought throughout the centuries are those that have been fought and won in the hearts of men and women of faith.

It's when you're standing against seemingly insurmountable barriers, that your faith is tested. That's the faith fight. When circumstances look impossible, you have to make a choice. Are you going to believe God and take Him at His Word — or are you going to believe the circumstances and allow your faith to crumble and fail?

The enemy will use every weapon he can against believers' faith. And one of the best weapons the enemy uses against people is deception through religious tradition and worldly teaching. If he can get our minds cluttered with the traditions of men, he can bring us into turmoil and confusion.

That's why we need to develop our faith according to God's Word, so we think like *God* thinks! When believers don't develop their faith so they can stand strong against the devil's strategies, their faith fizzles out. The

great revivalist D. L. Moody once said, "Faith that fizzles in the finish had a flaw in the beginning."

Possessing or Perishing?

So why are some believers missing it in being able
to possess their promised land? First, the Bible says
people perish because of lack of knowledge.

> **HOSEA 4:6**
> **6 My people are destroyed for lack of knowl-
> edge....**

Just because people are members of a church or
hear a message on faith or listen to teaching tapes is no
sign they have Bible knowledge. For one thing, they
may be hearing, but they may not be receiving.

Or they may be hearing with their mind, but not
with their heart. Or sometimes what they hear confuses
them because they haven't developed a relationship
with God the Father yet.

Many people who are in the move of God right now
upon the earth are excited about the things of God, and
they are interested in finding out about their benefits
in Christ.

They want to know what they can receive from God.
But because they haven't built a strong relationship
with Him, they really don't know how to go about
receiving what God has for them.

Build a Strong Relationship With God

Of course if it's in the proper perspective, it's all right to want to receive from God. But it's sad when believers go after the benefits of God and aren't even interested in establishing a relationship with Him.

These believers have a high expectation of faith — they want to receive all they can in this life with their faith. But they aren't willing to pay the price to establish their faith on a solid relationship with God. They need to get to know Him as their Heavenly *Father*.

It's great that their faith expectation is high, but they haven't learned the secret of seeking first the Kingdom of God and His righteousness.

The Bible says when we seek Him first, that's when all the other things — the benefits and blessings of God— are added to us (Matt. 6:33).

You won't be able to possess what God has for you unless you develop a strong relationship with your Heavenly Father. Without a relationship with Him, your faith will fizzle and perish.

Believers can be children of God but never develop their relationship with God, as a child to his father. In other words, they can be born again but never develop a relationship beyond their initial salvation experience.

Or sometimes they only develop a relationship with Him based on certain subjects like faith and prosperity. They only know about the subjects they enjoy, so those are the only subjects they kick up their heels at. Therefore, they really don't have a grasp of the whole counsel of God.

Also, many believers just run after the *benefits* of God instead of seeking the *Kingdom of God*, and it causes their faith to fizzle, sputter, and dry up. Then they wonder why their faith won't work for them!

Once their faith dries up, they develop a negative attitude about faith and complain that the principles of faith don't work for them. They cry, "Faith in the Word doesn't work! God failed to meet my needs!"

No, God didn't fail to meet their needs! God has never failed anyone on the face of this earth. That's impossible! But the problem is that without a close relationship with God, they don't have any foundation for their faith.

Because they don't really know God, they don't understand the principles of faith. They're born again, but they haven't grown in their relationship with God. Therefore, they can't grow in faith, because God is a *faith* God.

Arrogance or Boldness?

If you want strong faith, you need to know your Father God as a child knows his daddy. This is where you and I need to learn just to kneel down and begin to talk to our Heavenly Father just like we would talk to a loving earthly father.

Many believers have had the privilege to sit down and talk to a loving earthly father when things weren't going right. How wonderful to sit down with our earthly father and say, "Dad, I need to talk something over with you."

But you can do the same thing with your Heavenly Father. You can go to Him and say, "Father, I need to have a talk with you." When you develop that kind of a close relationship with God, it's easy to live in the promises of God! The God-kind of faith comes naturally when you know the God of faith!

When you have a proper relationship with God, you'll come to your Heavenly Father with a right attitude because you've developed a good, solid relationship with Him. You'll know how to boldly claim His promises without being arrogant.

On the other hand, some believers come into the Presence of God, and their relationship with their Heavenly Father is strained because they don't really know Him. Often they are full of fear. Why? Sometimes it's just that they need to learn how to fellowship with their Heavenly Father with the simplicity and trust of a little child.

There's something about entering into the throne room of God with the simple attitude of a child — pure, humble, and trusting. Jesus said we receive the Kingdom of God like a little child (Luke 18:17).

How many of you parents want to give your children the blessings they ask for when they come to you with a challenging, demanding attitude? It doesn't work, does it? Well, what makes us think we can do that with God?

You see, we need to approach our Heavenly Father with a meek, Christ-like attitude. Study how Jesus talked to His Father in His earth walk. He was bold, but never arrogant. Yet His prayers were always answered because He always had His Father's thoughts and desires uppermost in His mind.

Through the blood of Jesus, we are joint-heirs with Jesus Christ, the Son of God (Eph. 2:6). That makes Jesus' Heavenly Father our own Father, just as He is Jesus' Father. So we need to learn from Jesus' relationship with His Father God, so we can develop our own close relationship with God.

Lack of Knowledge
Causes Faith To Perish

The word "perish" is defined as *to destroy or ruin and eventually to die.* The Bible says that it's a lack of knowledge that causes people to be destroyed, and without knowledge their faith will eventually perish.

I'm concerned for believers that they really get ahold of the truth of God's Word about faith — not what they *think* faith is.

For instance, the message of faith in God's Word is *not* "Gimme, gimme, gimme! I want! I want! I want!" That's not the God-kind of faith.

But it seems that in our day all too often believers are only interested in getting, getting, getting! Even if they do give, some of them arrogantly say, "Well, I gave! Now, God, I *expect* a hundredfold return!"

"I give, so I expect." That's sad! Yes, expecting a return on your giving is part of Bible faith. Receiving a return on your giving is part of God's plan and His laws of prosperity. And if your attitude is right, that's one way you will receive from God.

But it's sad when believers are more concerned with *getting* than they are with *giving*. And it's sad when believers aren't interested in a close relationship with God — they're just interested in getting all of His benefits!

The point is that when a person gives with the wrong motive, his faith will eventually fizzle out because he doesn't have a solid relationship with God. If a person doesn't really *know* God, how can he understand the laws of God, including giving and receiving?

You see, when you have a right relationship with God, and you really know *Him*, then you become like Him. Then your main concern isn't what you're going to receive from your giving.

You're much more concerned about giving so people can be helped and blessed, because you're beginning to think the way God thinks. You give because you want to do what's right in God's sight and build up His Kingdom. And you give because you want to be in God's perfect will in every area of your life.

When the motives of your heart are pure, the benefits of God can really begin to come rolling in and overtake you in life. That's when you really start "eating the good of the land" and *living* in your abundant inheritance in Christ.

So many believers think they've got it made just because they've received some return on their giving. But they are really just living on the outer fringe of God's abundant blessings!

If they would forget about just running after the fringe benefits of their inheritance in Christ all the time and really take time to understand the truth of God's Word, how they would prosper in every area of life!

What should our attitude be about giving? Look in the Word and see what God's attitude is about giving. The Bible says, "God so *loved* the world, that He *gave* . . ." (John 3:16). God loves, so He gives. In other words, God's motive for giving was *love.*

That's the kind of giving that reaps rich dividends, not only in this life, but in the next life too! Giving that's motivated by love is giving with a right attitude, and it causes the blessings of God to be multiplied in your life.

When you give because you love God and you love the people of God, it's amazing how the promises of God start working for you. The benefits of God begin to overtake you in life.

I'm not against prosperity or giving. I'm for all the benefits that belong to us in Christ! But I'm talking about giving with a right attitude and a pure heart so it will benefit you for eternity!

Think about your own life. What's the attitude behind your giving? That's what God looks at. God can't honor your giving if it's from impure motives. Giving just to get so you can heap pleasures upon yourself hardly reflects the nature of God!

The kind of giving that pleases God comes from knowing *Him*. You know Him so well that His giving, loving character becomes part of your nature, and you can't help but give. You love to give!

I believe most Christians would be shocked at the blessings and benefits that would overtake them in life if they really understood how to operate the laws of giving from the motives of love and a right relationship with God. There would be no struggle to possess their promised land if they gave to the work of God out of love.

Let's give to others from the pure motive of love! Let's minister to others because of love, not out of necessity. Let's do everything from the motive of love, not because we have to, but because we *want* to. Then we're not only obedient, but willing. That's what pleases God.

I'm not just talking about money. I'm also talking about giving of ourselves to those in need — not because we know we'll get something in return — but because we want to bless, encourage, and help people.

Let's establish a relationship with God so that when we act in faith, we move and act by the will and the power of God. That's the God-kind of faith in demonstration. Then we won't act just motivated by "hyper" faith.

We may not even *feel* inspired, but we'll be motivated to do things for others and give to them because we're God's children, created in His likeness. His desire to love and give becomes our desire too.

As God's children, our mission in life is to give. If we have a giving attitude in everything we do in life, the windows of Heaven will open for us. The blessings of God will pour upon us so abundantly, we won't be able to contain them.

It Takes Humility To Prosper in God

Humility is one way to possess all the promises of God in your life. Humility is one of the fruits of a right relationship with God. The Bible says humility causes us to be exalted in due season and to prosper.

> **1 PETER 5:6**
> **6   Humble yourselves therefore under the mighty hand of God, that he may exalt you in due time.**

Humility is walking with God in all godliness and integrity, knowing that you are nothing without God. The Bible promises that when you really walk before God with true humility of heart, God will exalt you in due season. What does "in due season" mean? It means when you're mature enough to handle it!

We know that without God and the blood of the Lord Jesus Christ we are unworthy. Everything we are and everything we possess comes from God Himself.

Sometimes the reason our faith confessions and all our giving fall short is that we're not humble, so God can't exalt us. If we're not humble, we fail to realize how dependent we are on God. Sometimes we just aren't humble enough to receive the blessings of God!

Some people never humble themselves enough to realize that they can do nothing in their own strength.

They become so prideful that they take credit for all the blessings and achievements in their life. Because their thinking is wrong, they allow the devil to come in, and they ultimately fall and their faith fizzles out.

Some people get over on the other side of that ditch though. They think they're too unworthy to receive anything from God, including their inheritance in Christ. But God has never made an unworthy new creature.

Remember, Ephesians 4:24 says, ". . . *put on the new man, which after God is created in righteousness and true holiness.*" That doesn't sound like an unworthy person, does it?

Actually, to say that you are unworthy is to speak against God because you're speaking against God's new creation — you!

When we became new creatures in Christ, we became worthy because the blood of Jesus cleansed us from all iniquity. Without the blood of Jesus Christ, none of us is worthy.

Some believers get confused and can't distinguish between unworthiness and humility. They think if they feel unworthy, they are being humble before God. But if people really understood godly humility, they would get a lot further with God.

True humility before God is recognizing that at all times without God in our lives, we are totally insufficient and inadequate in life. That's godly humility!

But many believers get so puffed up in themselves, they think *they* are the ones responsible for their own accomplishments and achievements in life. And they can really get arrogant, and sometimes they even think they can tell God what to do.

You see, sometimes there's just a fine line between humility and unworthiness, and boldness and arrogance. But some people push beyond that line and actually overstep it.

They think they're being bold when really they're being arrogant. Or they think they are being humble, but they're really acting like they're unworthy of God's blessings. But you'll need *both* humility and boldness in their proper perspectives to inherit your promised land!

Yes, as children of God, we possess certain covenant rights. But the problem is the way that some believers act before their Heavenly Father, arrogantly demanding those covenant rights. We're not going to be able to possess our promised land if our attitudes are wrong.

Now get ahold of what I'm saying. I'm not saying that we can't talk to God or boldly come into His Presence to state our needs and claim His promises. He is our Heavenly Father, so of course we can. God invites us to remind Him of what His Word says (Isa. 43:26). And God is faithful to honor His Word.

However, it's all in our attitude of heart. How do we come before the throne of grace? Like all things, there's a right way and a wrong way to approach God.

Some believers come boldly before God to put Him in remembrance of His Word, but they lack godly attitudes, so God can't bless them like He wants to.

It's time we believers realized that there are two sides to faith. Yes, there is the strong faith stance that boldly puts God in remembrance of His Word. But then there's the balance of faith too. That means your faith has to be built on a strong relationship with God, and it also has to be founded on humility and godliness.

Believers can get so excited about operating in faith principles that they forget about the balance to faith, which includes godly attitudes and holy living. The Bible says that faith works by *love* (Gal. 5:6).

It's time for us to realize that the blessings of God come from holy living, not *just* from faith confessions. One of our United States Presidents said something that Christians need to heed. He said, "Don't ask what your country can do for *you*; ask what you can do for your *country*."

It's time some of us forget about what God can do for us and concentrate on what we can do for God! When that kind of servant's attitude of love really gets down in our heart — talk about possessing what belongs to us in Christ! We'll walk into a life of abundance without even realizing how we got there!

Right Attitudes Draw You Nigh to God

We need to get our attitudes and our actions in line with the Word of God. Then watch the Word work! Some believers' *actions* are in line with God's Word, but they've neglected to get their *attitudes* in line with it.

The Bible says it's the little foxes that spoil the vine

(Song of Sol. 2:15). Many times it's the little attitudes we never deal with that cause us problems when we want to tackle something big like possessing the promises of God for our lives.

Sometimes wrong attitudes are hidden from our view, and we don't recognize them for what they are right away. For example, the Bible says, *"If ye be willing AND obedient, ye shall eat the good of the land"* (Isa. 1:19).

A lot of people are obedient to the Word of God, but they really don't practice it from a willing heart. When they aren't willing and their attitude is wrong in the sight of God, even though they're a doer of the Word, they won't be able to prosper.

That's where a strong relationship with God the Father comes in. When you walk closely with your Heavenly Father, you can talk to Him about those areas where your heart is not willing. And He'll help you become willing to do His will in every area of life. Then you can really be the success God wants you to be.

Parents can always tell when their children are being obedient, but not willing. Then sometimes they have to deal with their children's attitudes to really get them on the right track of obedience.

That's where a lot of Christians are today. God wants to deal with their attitudes to get them on track with Him so He can bless them abundantly. He wants their attitudes right before Him so He can give them everything He has for them in this life.

You see, the Word of God possesses in itself the

power to bring to pass whatever you need. Wrapped up in God's Word is all-sufficient power.

The power in God's Word contains the one-hundred-percent guaranteed ability to bring to pass God's promises in your life.

So there's no lack of ability or power with the Word. If there's any lack, it's with us! And sometimes the problem is that only a small portion of the Word of God really *abides* in our heart.

I'm not talking about head knowledge about the Word — I'm talking about heart knowledge! When we don't have much of the Word in our heart, the enemy is able to easily get us into confusion or disobedience.

And Satan has many believers running scared in some areas of their lives because they don't know who they are in Christ and what they possess in Christ. That should not be! There's more power in the Word of God than we could ever possibly tap into in a lifetime!

Reap the Rich Benefits of Commitment

Let's look at another thought in First Peter 5. You won't be able to possess what God has promised you if you're dragging the cares of this world around with you! You'll be so loaded down with cares, your faith will fizzle and eventually perish.

1 PETER 5:7
7   Casting all your care upon him; for he careth for you.

Why does God want you to cast your cares on Him and commit them to Him? Because He's big enough to deal with them — you're not! You won't be able to enter into the faith fight for your promised land with the cares of life weighing you down. Cast them on God, so your faith can be effectual.

Psalm 34:5 tells us something else that will help us in the good fight of faith. It says, *"Commit thy way unto the Lord; trust also in him; and he shall bring it to pass."* We have to do the *committing*, then God will bring His promises to pass.

Who is going to bring to pass the promises of God in our lives? The Lord! But we also have a part to play.

Some people fizzle out and their faith perishes because they miss one little word in that scripture. That word is "commit." That one little word shows you how strong or how weak your relationship is with God.

We not only have to commit our *cares* to God so He can work them out, we also have to commit *ourselves* to Him so we can follow Him wholly.

Many believers want to possess the promises of God, but they don't want to commit to anything. Oh, they want God's best blessings in life, all right. But they don't want to make any commitments to God to get them!

But find any promise in God's Word, and I'll show you the other side of that promise. The other side of the promise is the commitment it takes on your part to cooperate with God so He can bring that promise to pass in your life. You will have to be obedient and committed to God before you can inherit the promises of God.

All the promises of God are based on commitment and obedience. It's your commitment to God and His Word that will enable God to work on your behalf and bring His promises to pass in your life.

Many times in the Word, God says, "If *you* do this, *I* will do this." We have our responsibility, and God has His. Our responsibility is to obey. Once God sees our obedience, it's easy for Him to bring His part of the plan to pass!

You even had to be obedient to even get saved. You had to believe the Word and receive Jesus Christ as your Savior. And once you were born again, the benefits, rights, and privileges of your redemption were also made available to you.

For example, one *benefit* of salvation is that you receive everlasting life. But you also have certain *responsibilities* in your salvation. You have to live for God. That takes commitment on your part.

Really, it takes commitment to be a success in any area of life. But do you know what's wrong with many believers? They want to possess *everything* God has for them, but they don't want to make a commitment to *anything*. They just want to go through life, floating from one faith adventure to another, just enjoying a good ole time.

But if you don't commit yourself to God and His Word, you won't receive God's best blessings in life. It's that simple.

Talking about Christian commitment reminds me of a story about a chicken and a pig who were walking down a country road one day. They came across a fellow who was hungry.

The chicken smiled and said to the pig, "Let's give him some ham and eggs." But the pig squealed, "No way! That would take a hundred-percent commitment on my part!"

You see, it wouldn't take much of a commitment on the chicken's part to provide some eggs, but it would take a total commitment on the pig's part to provide some ham!

Sometimes Christians are like that chicken. As long as there's no commitment involved, they're in favor of it. It's easy to sing loud and long and to dance and jump and get hilarious as long as no one talks about commitment to God.

People love to get excited about the benefits — all the great things God is doing for them. But let someone start talking about the total commitment it takes to sell out completely to God, and people get quiet in a hurry!

When you start preaching on commitment and the believer's responsibility, people complain, "Aw, preacher! You're preaching negatively!"

But until you know what your responsibility is to receive God's blessings, you won't be able to fulfill it. You can make all the faith confessions you want to, but until you've made a total commitment to God, God can't honor all your wonderful faith confessions.

Many times when you preach about faith, healing, and prosperity, people are in total agreement with you because they love to hear teaching on those subjects.

But you start talking about commitment and consecration, and they don't want to hear about it. However, those subjects come from the pages of God's Word too!

This is one reason why people fizzle out in their faith and can't possess what rightfully belongs to them. They never learned how to stand on God's Word in these other areas too. They only learned how to fight the good fight of faith for certain benefits they like, such as faith, healing, and prosperity. And that's fine as far as it goes.

However, there are other scriptures in God's Word that need to be part of our faith and lifestyle, too, so we can grow up in Christ. We'll have to fight the good fight of faith to be successful in those areas too.

I am not downgrading faith, healing, or prosperity. I had the privilege of being raised in a man's home where we had to learn how to fight the good fight of faith in every area of our Christian lives.

My father, Rev. Kenneth E. Hagin, learned as a teenager how to believe God for healing, and as my sister and I were growing up, he taught us about faith for healing. But we also had to learn from the Word how to fight the good fight of faith to get our needs met, because sometimes there wasn't enough to eat!

For example, I remember one time in 1957, my dad was holding meetings out in California. It was in the summertime, and the whole family was traveling with Dad.

We went to the service every night wearing the best we had. No one knew that we didn't have any money or that we were eating one meal a day and that was a can of beans and some fried potatoes. That's all we had and even that ran out.

We never told anyone our need. We just agreed together and thanked God for what we did have. We ate what we had, and thanked God in faith that every need was met.

But one morning a fellow rang the doorbell of that travel trailer we were staying in. This man said to Dad, "Brother Hagin, I didn't even know you were in this part of the country. But the Lord woke me up this morning about four o'clock and told me where you were and the name of the trailer park you were staying in. He told me that you didn't have any groceries."

Then he said, "I've got a pickup load of groceries out here in my truck for you."

Dad just smiled and said, "I don't doubt it, praise God."

I've seen that happen time and time again. But, you see, things like that wouldn't have happened if we hadn't been totally committed to God.

Yes, sometimes your commitment will be tested. But stand true to God. Don't throw your faith away, and God will always see you through.

But I'm going to tell you something. You may endure some trials as you take your promised land. It won't always be easy. *You* are going to have to be totally committed to what the Lord has told you to do if you're going to possess your land. But if you'll just commit yourself to God's plan, He will make sure you possess what He's promised you.

Renew Your Mind — So *You* Can Be Transformed

1 CORINTHIANS 2:16
16 For who hath known the mind of the Lord, that he may instruct him? But WE HAVE THE MIND OF CHRIST.

PHILIPPIANS 2:5
5   LET THIS MIND BE IN YOU, which was also in Christ Jesus.

Do you want to know one way to make sure you possess your promised land? Renew your mind with the promises of God. The Word of God tells us that believers are to have the mind of Christ.

The Amplified Bible explains what that means. First Corinthians 2:16 says, ". . . we have the mind of Christ, the Messiah, and do hold the thoughts (feelings and purposes) of His heart."

Believers who fulfill the promises of God for their life renew their minds so they can have the mind and attitude of Christ. Then whatever they do, they do because of the love of God so they can benefit others. That's one reason why they receive the benefits of their covenant with God.

Jesus Christ always kept His mind on His Heavenly Father. He always abided in fellowship with God the Father. That's why it wasn't difficult for Jesus to always want to do His Father's will.

Jesus never considered His own will first because His mind was always fixed on pleasing God and putting the will of God the Father first. He didn't consider Himself, but He considered God first and then others.

If we want our minds to be in line with the mind of Christ, then we'll have to practice Romans 12:2: *"Be ye transformed by the renewing of your mind."* This scripture needs to become a lifestyle with us! If we get our *mind* transformed, *we* will be transformed.

To a large extent, your mind determines whether or not you receive what God has for you in life. You won't be able to receive your promised land with an unrenewed mind and negative thinking.

So many people just emphasize the work of the Holy Spirit in obtaining the promises of God. And, yes, the Holy Spirit should be reverenced and honored. But many times they don't realize the part they play in cooperating with the Holy Spirit by keeping their own mind renewed.

You have a responsibility to possess what God has promised you, and it is something the Holy Spirit can't do for you. You'll have to get your natural mind renewed with the Word of God. It's a lot easier for the Holy Spirit to work through your mind when it's been renewed by the Word of God!

It's so much easier for the Holy Spirit to work

through you in every situation in life when your mind has been dwelling on the Word. That's especially true in the crises of life.

If you've put the Word in your heart, then in times of trouble, your mind immediately begins to think on the Word instead of dwelling on the problem. The power of the Word flowing through your mind opens the door for the Holy Spirit to take over and flood you with His peace and joy and give you direction in the midst of trouble.

In a sense, we're in partnership with God in obtaining His promises. But so many believers want to forget about their responsibility — what they are to do with their own mind and body.

It seems like they want the Holy Spirit to take all the responsibility for their success. They act like they're waiting for the Holy Spirit to somehow supernaturally *cause* them to inherit all the promises of God, so they don't have to put forth much effort.

But it will take some effort and commitment on your part to inherit God's promises to you — your own personal promised land. You won't be able to do it without getting your mind renewed so you think in line with God's thinking.

We're quick to quote, *"For as many as are led by the Spirit of God, they are the sons of God"* (Rom. 8:14). But often we don't much like to quote Romans 12:2: *". . . be not conformed to this world: but be ye transformed by the renewing of your mind. . . ."*

Of course, we need to establish a strong relationship with the Holy Spirit, so we can know how to follow

Him. But we also need to get back to the whole counsel of God's Word. God's Word will tell you the part that *you* play in your own success.

The Bible says to renew your mind with the Word so you are not conformed to this world. *Then* you will be able to prove what is the good, acceptable, and perfect will of God for your life (Rom. 12:1,2).

According to this scripture, we don't just know the will of God from our spirit; we can also know it from our renewed mind. How can that be? Because there are some things we don't even need to ask God about. His Word tells us what His will is, and when our mind is renewed, we just know right from wrong.

Believers are always wanting to know what the will of God is for their lives. It seems like Christians get confused and fizzle out in their faith over this one question probably more than almost any other issue.

But we don't need to stumble about knowing the will of God for our lives. Just stay in close fellowship with God and get your mind renewed with His Word, and you'll know what to do in every situation in life.

The reason most believers don't know the *will* of God is that they are ignorant about the *Word* of God. Many of them only renew their minds on a few subjects like faith, healing, and prosperity. And those are some of our benefits in Christ.

But many of them never renew their minds in other areas of the Word of God such as rightstanding with God, judgment, consecration, and their relationship with their Heavenly Father.

You won't be able to hold the thoughts, feelings, and purposes of God's heart unless you are in the Word. And sometimes it will take more willpower to study some Bible subjects that aren't all that inspiring, like consecration and commitment!

For one thing, when you study the Word, you'll find out that you've carried around a lot of little idiosyncrasies and habits as excess spiritual baggage, and you have to get rid of them. You'll just have to cut off sin and the weights that try to entangle you. It's not the Holy Spirit who cuts off sin. *You* do.

Once you know what God's Word says about something, then you just have to quit doing it. No one said it's going to be easy to crucify the flesh. But if you want to be able to possess all that God has for you, you'll have to learn to do it, or your flesh will hinder you from making spiritual progress.

Why do you think Jesus used the illustration of cutting off a hand or plucking out an eye (Matt. 5:29,30)? He was talking about dealing with the flesh! We have to crucify the flesh, and sometimes it hurts so much, it's like cutting off our hand or plucking out our eye!

It's not any fun to judge ourselves, is it? But God promises us that if we judge ourselves, *He* won't have to. If we don't judge ourselves and put away the sins of the flesh, there's no way we're going to walk in God's best on this earth.

You'll have to learn to crucify the flesh if you want to walk in the abundance of your inheritance in Christ. But believers don't usually want to talk about keeping the flesh under because it's not inspiring. There's no hilarity to it! But it's still the Word of God, and God wants us to do it so we can succeed spiritually in life.

Another reason you need to renew your mind is that you're not always going to be in the Spirit in this life here on earth. If you could be sure the Holy Spirit would move on you in a spectacular way every time you went through a difficult situation, then you wouldn't need to study the Word and get your mind renewed. Of course, we always have the abiding Presence of the Holy Spirit on the inside of us because we're born again.

But, for example, if you're working on your car, and the wrench slips and you accidentally smash your hand, you can't be sure the Spirit of God is going to come upon you mightily! However, you *can* do something with your own flesh so you won't get mad and say or do things you'll regret.

What do you do with your flesh? You begin quoting all those beautiful verses in God's Word. That helps you keep your flesh under. But if you don't have the Word in your mind and in your heart, you won't be able to control your flesh so easily.

Of course, sometimes God does move supernaturally by His Spirit. But it's as the Spirit wills, and you won't necessarily always know when He's going to move supernaturally upon you.

That's why you're going to have to manifest the Word of God in your flesh by being filled up with God's all-powerful Word! Then when something goes wrong, you can begin declaring, "Bless God! The Word of God says . . ." That's how you produce a harvest of blessing in your life!

Quote God's Word over your situation: "No weapon formed against me shall prosper" (Isa. 54:17). "All the promises of God are yea and amen in Christ" (2 Cor. 1:20). "Thanks be to God, who gives me the victory through our Lord Jesus Christ" (1 Cor. 15:57). "In all things I am more than a conqueror through Him who loves me" (Rom. 8:37).

You see, the greatest weapon we possess in any situation is the Word. But we have to use the Word for it to be effective. Let's go on to victory and joy! Let's go on to the greatest and the best blessings of God by putting His Word to work for us!

The Word of God belongs to the child of God. Actually, the Word is the believer's most prized possession! It's his weapon to stand strong against the enemy and his devices.

The Word tells the believer how to appropriate the rights and privileges of his covenant, and how to come boldly, yet humbly before his Heavenly Father.

Let's get on track with God's Word. With all our hearts, let's seek the Kingdom of God first and His righteousness. Then we can find out what pleases God so we can walk in close fellowship to Him.

Walking in close fellowship with God is how you scripturally possess your promised land. Find out for yourself what it means to fight the good fight of faith with the Word of God. Then possess what belongs to you so that you can take back what the devil's stolen, and bring it into the Kingdom of God where it belongs!

Think about it! Any child would get upset if he saw someone stealing something from his earthly father, wouldn't he? His first thought would be to go get it back. As God's children, when we see the enemy sticking up his ugly head stealing from the Kingdom of God, we should have the same determination as the Lord Jesus Christ to get it back for God!

It Takes the Whole Counsel of God's Word To Possess God's Promises

A lot of believers think they can walk this Christian walk successfully just by learning how to develop their spirit. Yes, that is a part of spiritual success. But we just need to get back to the whole counsel of God's Word.

Think about it. It's not your spirit that comes into contact with this world we live in; your spirit comes into contact with the supernatural realm. Your mind and body come into contact with this world. In this world, it's your physical body that bumps its knee or stubs its toe.

When you're playing in sports, and you get knocked around, it's your body that gets hurt, and it's your flesh nature that wants to rise up and get mad. If it were your spirit out there contacting the world, your spirit man would always know how to walk in love.

But it's not your spirit man that contacts the world. Your spirit contacts the spiritual realm. Your physical, natural body and your mind are conscious of this world we live in.

But when your mind is renewed with the Word of God, you're transformed so that when you face trials in this world, the Word comes out of your mouth. And when you speak the Word, that releases the Holy Spirit to help you overcome *any* situation. That's what gives you the strength to keep your flesh from sinking into despair.

That's one reason some believers aren't overcomers and never possess what God has for them. When they get in the middle of a crisis, they don't know enough of the Word of God to get out of the problem!

They can't release faith-filled words from their *mouth* because they haven't taken time to put God's faith-filled Word in their *heart*. As a result, they can't find a way out of their situation.

If we'll get our minds renewed with the Word of God, and get our attitudes in line with the Word, we won't have to worry about our faith fizzling out and eventually perishing. We'll enjoy the victory and the possession of the promises of God.

Really, what I'm talking about is spiritual maturity. The Body of Christ so desperately needs maturity in Christ in this hour so we can possess our promised land and prosper in every area of life.

The benefits of our inheritance in Christ will come rolling in if we'll just get our attitudes right with God. If we'll just manifest the love of God, it won't be a problem to live in the rich blessings of God.

The love of God can't be expressed by selfish attitudes. The attitude, *What am I going to get out of it!* isn't a problem to those who fellowship with their Heavenly Father so they love to give like He does. When believers walk in God's love, they'll love to give too. For God so loved, that He gave.

But I am disturbed at the attitudes of some believers in our day. I see a lot of people who have gotten selfish with their faith.

It bothers me that so many believers have gotten ahold of the Word of God and have become so selfish with it. They say, "I'm believing God for this," and "I'm believing God for that." "God give me this!" or "God give me that." But it's all for selfish motives!

I've talked to some believers who were continually talking about all the *things* they'd believed God for such as a new car, a new house, or a new ministry building. They were selfish with their faith because they only prayed for themselves and their own needs to be met.

Many times when I talk to believers like that, I ask them one question. Maybe it gets them thinking. I ask them, "How many people have you used your faith to lead to Jesus Christ recently?"

Now there's nothing wrong with believing God for our needs to be met. But if that's *all* we use our faith for, there's something wrong!

You see, God wants to bring a great revival upon this earth. He wants to step across every church threshold with His power and glory. He wants to bring people together in the unity of His Spirit in a great dimension in our day. But as long as believers just use their faith selfishly for their own desires, they can hinder what God really wants to do in the world today.

Revival Fires Burn Brightly Through Pure Vessels

Study the history of revivals throughout the centuries. In every revival, as long as believers' number-one priority was the love of God and reaching out to a lost and dying world, the revival fires of the Holy Spirit burned brightly. And God used believers who were on fire for Him mightily to His glory.

But when people got selfish or just became concerned about blessing their own denomination or their own little group, the revival began to wane and eventually die out.

That's what's happening right now in our day. Many believers are selfishly trying to use the power of God just for their own personal benefit.

Unless we shake ourselves and really begin to preach the truth of God's Word and stand up with spiritual maturity and teach people the power of the Word to benefit others, God will be hindered from moving in the magnitude He desires on this earth.

Thank God for all of the benefits of our redemption. Our inheritance in Christ is great and glorious, and we're thankful for it. But we need to stir ourselves up in our first love, and stay in rich fellowship with our precious Heavenly Father so we can win a world for Christ.

We need to stir ourselves up with the pure fervency to tell the world about *Jesus*. We need to give of ourselves, our time, our money — not for any personal gain we might receive — but for the sheer love of giving to build up the Kingdom of God.

I believe this God we serve can do anything. Nothing is impossible with Him. As far as I'm concerned, that's just a fact!

But I also see something that stirs me to my very bones. It's going to take a pure faith in God to get the job done on the earth that God is requiring. It's going to take the God-kind of faith to activate the power of God. A faith that's motivated by selfishness is *not* going to move God!

I've grown up in the household of faith. I've never known anything else but living by this faith in a God who knows that nothing is impossible with Him.

And I know that God will never stand for selfish, impure motives in our faith walk — not if we're going to have the kind of faith that's going to take the world for Jesus!

I've seen ministries in days gone by fail and fall by the wayside because they became selfish and wanted to heap the blessings of God upon themselves for selfish purposes and personal ambition.

My heart cry to the Body of Christ today is that none of us would be guilty of allowing our faith to fizzle out and perish just because it wasn't founded upon a firm foundation — pure motives and a strong relationship with God.

We won't be able to keep our faith strong if we are more concerned with our own wants and needs than we are to reach out and help others. Our faith will fizzle and eventually perish, and we'll wonder what happened.

But when you reach out to others with the love of God, just watch God make sure you succeed so you can help *many* others! It's by God's Word that we overcome every difficulty in life.

God is our great and mighty Refuge and Provider. We will know no lack when we choose to love the way He loves. So shall He reward us openly.

You see, the enemy cannot kill the power of God. He cannot stop the mighty move of God upon this earth. There's no way the devil can stop the move of God's Spirit from bringing revival to this earth.

But the devil can hinder the move of God when the believer takes the power that is in faith and turns it inward so it becomes selfish. Anything that feeds upon itself will become stale, stagnant, and eventually die.

Once faith becomes stagnant, it will begin to stink. And without the proper motivation of love, faith will eventually fizzle out and decay, because it's not producing anything.

But with God's life and love flowing in us by the power of the Holy Spirit, we don't have to become stagnant and weak in faith. Our faith doesn't have to fizzle and perish.

We can make sure our faith stays strong by getting

back to the principles of the love of God. We can develop the God-kind of faith by turning our love and faith outward to help and benefit others. To do that we'll have to forget about ourselves.

Let's think about a world that's lost and dying and use our faith to take a strong stand on the Word of God against the enemy of God.

With our faith in God, let's set people free! Using the same faith that taught us how to get our needs met, let's go out and teach others how to get free and *stay* free!

God desires to demonstrate his power in our lifetime in a way that we've never seen before. If we'll work with Him and His principles of giving from a heart of love, He'll accomplish all that He desires through us, His Body, on the earth.

God can only demonstrate His power through us as we take the love of God, the power of God, and the faith of God that we've learned to help others. So let's use our faith to bring what belongs to God into the Kingdom of God — souls for God's glory.

Really, the question is, What do you want in life? Do you want to bring many souls into the Kingdom of God? Or do you just want to live this life for yourself?

The highest goal you could ever have in this life is to help others. And as you help others attain their dreams in God, you are helping further the Kingdom of God on this earth.

God has given to each one of us our own dreams and

desires — our own promised land. We need to fulfill those dreams and desires so God can be glorified in our lives.

Everything you need to fulfill your God-given dreams and heart's desire are contained in the pages of God's Word. But as you help someone else attain their promised land, you'll help yourself realize your own dreams too.

For some of you, the devil has almost stolen your promised land from you. He's tried to rob you of the promises of God for your life.

Some of you just need to rise up and begin declaring, "No devil is going to steal my joy! No devil is going to steal what God promised me. Satan, in Jesus' Name I won't allow you to take my promised land from me!"

Realize that you aren't waiting on God to receive your promised land. God is waiting on you! Through Jesus Christ, He has richly provided everything you will ever need in this life to be a success.

Don't just look and long for those blessings God has already provided for you in this life. Look to God's Word with faith in your heart. Begin to speak the promises of God out of your mouth. Speak to every mountain of hindrance in your life. Move them out of your way!

Releasing faith in God's Word activates the power of God in your life. Then as you help others attain their dreams in God, you, too, can go in and possess the land that belongs to you! You can possess the mountain of your inheritance in Christ!